THE HIDDEN CURRICULUM

Practical Solutions for Understanding Unstated Rules in Social Situations

D0870988

More Advance Praise . . .

"Finally a book that spells out the 'real' rules of social conduct, not just how to be polite. The great advantage of this book is that it delineates guidelines for children and teens to follow that are specific to the real-life situations in which they typically interact. This is an essential reference tool for anyone who is living or working with students with social-communication difficulties."

Jed Baker, Ph.D., Director, Social Skills Training Project in New Jersey
Author, Social Skills Training for Children and Adolescents with Asperger Syndrome and Social-Communication Disorders

"The Hidden Curriculum is an excellent resource for teachers and parents who are striving to create meaningful social skills lessons for their students who have difficulty interpreting social information. The hidden curriculum is an elusive concept, and this book does an excellent job of not only defining it, but offering clear suggestions for how to teach it."

Kari Dunn Buron, M.S.
Author, The Incredible 5-Point Scale *and* When My Autism Gets Too Big!

"This is the first book I have seen addressing in a practical way the unspoken rules of social engagement. In addition to providing a window into how people with Asperger Syndrome interpret their environment, the authors present to people with Asperger's how to navigate those mysterious cues emitted by body language and the uncharted areas of meaning "between the words."

Stephen M. Shore
Author, Beyond the Wall: Personal Experiences with Autism and Asperger Syndrome
Editor, Ask and Tell: Self-Advocacy and Disclosure for People on the Autism Spectrum
Board President, Asperger's Association of New England

THE HIDDEN CURRICULUM

Practical Solutions for Understanding Unstated Rules in Social Situations

Brenda Smith Myles, Melissa L. Trautman, and Ronda L. Schelvan

Foreword by Michelle Garcia Winner

Autism Asperger Publishing Co.
P.O. Box 23173
Shawnee Mission, KS 66283-0173
www.asperger.net

© 2004 Autism Asperger Publishing Co.
P.O. Box 23173
Shawnee Mission, KS 66283-0173
www.asperger.net

All rights reserved. No part of the material protected by this copyright notice may be reproduced or used in any form or by any means, electronic or mechanical, including photocopying, recording, or by any information storage and retrieval system, without the prior written permission of the copyright owner.

Publisher's Cataloging-in-Publication
(Provided by Quality Books, Inc.)

Myles, Brenda.
    The hidden curriculum : practical solutions for
understanding unstated rules in social situations/
Brenda Myles, Melissa Trautman, and Ronda Schelvan.
    p. cm.
    Includes bibliographical references.
    Library of Congress Control Number: 2004108339
    ISBN 1-931282-60-9

    1. Social skills--Study and teaching.   I. Trautman,
Melissa. II. Schelvan, Ronda. III. Title.

HM691.M95 2004   302'.14
                  QB104-200245

This book is designed in Funstuff, Helvetica and Palatino

Managing Editor: Kirsten McBride
Editorial Assistance: Ginny Biddulph

Printed in the United States of America

DEDICATION

We would like to thank the following individuals who contributed hidden curriculum items to this book while completing graduate coursework in autism spectrum disorders. Their commitment to individuals with social-cognitive challenges, including Asperger Syndrome, is commendable. This book is dedicated to them.

Jennifer Adair
Carol Affolder
Katie Alexander
Andrea Anderson
Susan Anderson
Aida Ayala-Olivarez
Shana Ayers
Gena Barnhill
Amy Beaver
Judy Becker
Linda Becker
Nicole Benoit
Gayle Bergstrand
Susana Bernad-Ripoll
Shelia Biggs
Patricia Bleish
Monica Bollier
Bobbi Bond
Rhonda Bowen
Dana Bowersock
Megan Brick
Kathy Brodie
Tierney Brown
Erika Buessing
Dawn Bullock
Lisa Burch
Anna Butler
Deborah Byrne
Carrie Calloway
Katherine Campbell
Cindy Carrigan
Rebecca Clark-
Hermocillo
Annelizabeth Cole
Tina Cole
Janice Cooley
Terri Cooper

Mary Alice Corn
Tina Cornell
Staci Crabtree
Heidi Cromwell
Jennifer Cross
Angie Dalbello
Sandy Davalos
Eileen Davis
Meagan Davis
Mary DiMarco
Theresa Duffy
Kathy Delmond
Sarah Dettmer
Kathleen Dewolfe
Lislie Dorrell
Melanie Dunagan
Julia Duval
Marla Eck
Elaine Fasulo
Heather Ferguson
Kathleen Flinn
Luz Forero
Denise Fraley
Mark Fraley
Shelley Francis
Janet Gertsner
Beverly Gieszelmann
Amanda Gosney
Laura Green
Taku Hagiwara
Sarah Hannibal
Heather Hanzlick
Melanie Harms
June Hayworth
Rebekah Heinrichs
Darlene Hoge
Caren Howes

Anastasia Hubbard
Jill Hudson
Abby Huggins
Rebecca Hughes
Carla Huhtanen
Janice Jenkins
Ketti Johnson-Coffelt
Tyi-Sanna Jones
Candace King
Paul LaCava
Wanda Lee
Jennifer Levenson
Alyssa Linn
Tara Livingston
Robert McCray
Saundra Manley
Stacey Martin
Kerry Mehaffey
Nancy Michael
Bruce Milford
Nancy Miller
Lisa Mims
Cathy Moseley
Michele Mullendore
Angela Murphy
Erica Neal
Kristine Newcomer
Bridget Newman
Spencer Nolan
Stephany Orr
Hye Ran Park
Mary Peacock
Candace Peters
Bess Powers
Kelly Prestia
Kara Radin
Nicole Rahaim

Jana Rejba
Louann Rinner
Jaime Rivetts
Lisa Robbins
Jacqueline Rogers
Maleia Rome
Mendy Ruthrauff
Jessica Saiter
Susie Sander
Christine Schang
Amy Schapman
Elesa Schmidt
Linda Scott
Rochelle Spicer
Stephanie Stansberry
Lee Stickle
Heather Stoehr
Hsein Su
Jodi Sundquist
Melissa Tate
Kelly Tebbenkamp
Lisa Toler
Shari Walker
Barbara Weatherford
Amy Weed
Jodi White
Shannyn Wilcoxson
Michelle Winburn
Lisa Wimberley
Lori Wood
Kathleen Wright
Kelly Yeokum
Amy Zegers
Kristie Ziegler

TABLE OF CONTENTS

Foreword

Social intuition is the lifeline that saves most of us on a daily basis from an array of potentially disastrous social situations. It also helps us navigate situations that could be physically or mentally harmful. Without realizing it, neurotypical folks constantly, instantaneously and seamlessly survey the unwritten rules or "hidden curriculum" of every environment and every person they encounter to make decisions about how to proceed successfully within a given context. This unconscious social navigator is one of the keys to having good "social skills."

Because good "social skills" generally emerge in neurotypical children with relatively minor effort and minimal coaching from parents and teachers, we take it for granted that all smart people should be able to acquire these naturally. However, within the last 10 years we have begun to acknowledge and explore the fact that there is a group of people who often demonstrate solid to exceptionally strong cognitive and language skills but have difficulties intuiting and adjusting socially to the very sensitive and unstated rules and emotions in everyday environments. These people have "social-cognitive learning disabilities."

This type of learning disability can be confusing to diagnosticians since it tends to encompass a variety of diagnostic labels, including autism, pervasive developmental disorder-not otherwise specified, Asperger Syndrome, nonverbal learning disability, attention deficit hyperactivity disorder, attention deficit disorder, semantic pragmatic disorder, and hyperlexia. It also includes many with Tourette's Syndrome, sensory integration disorder, executive functioning disability and emotional disturbances, as well as a number of others who have no clear diagnostic label.

Those of us who work closely with persons with social-cognitive learning disabilities recognize that their inability to develop social skills and interpret the social nuances of those around them brings deep and lifelong challenges that impact their lives in a multitude of ways, including socially, emotionally, behaviorally, recreationally and vocationally. It is also important to recognize how personal safety and decision making can be at risk if people are not able to quickly and efficiently adapt to and read social cues and intuit the hidden rules that surround them at every turn.

The good news for people with social-cognitive learning disabilities is that help is on the way! Professionals dedicated to exploring the depth and complexity of what constitutes "social skills" are making tremendous strides in our ability to recognize and develop effective strategies to promote what I refer to as "social thinking." To work with persons with social-cognitive deficits proactively and successfully, educators and parents must be "social anthropologists." For example, on a recent trip to a bookstore, I worked with a client to determine some of the "hidden curriculum" items within the store by exploring how many different sets of rules exist under that one roof. We found that there were at least nine different sets! There were rules to adjust your voice and body as soon as you walk through the doors to enter the store; rules for standing in line at the counter; rules for being in the coffee shop and even more rules for ordering food in the coffee shop; rules for how to behave in the magazine section, children's section, music section, and general book store section; there were even rules for sitting in the section with the big comfy chairs. Thus, to be considered socially appropriate within this one store means that you constantly have to adjust your social behavior to the demands of these "hidden rules." By comparison, imagine how many sets of unwritten rules exist within a school day, for example!

This book by Brenda Smith Myles, Melissa Trautman and Ronda Schelvan is a critical tool for helping us all learn more about the hidden social information (e.g., hidden curriculum) that we must analyze in order to be better parents and educators. The analysis provided in the "lists of curriculum items" chapter is just the tip of the iceberg and serves as a jumping-off point for our own analysis of various situations and their social rules. As much as I have thought about the hidden curriculum, this book provides even further food for thought in its exploration of how elusive, dynamic and transient this information is. The gold nugget in this book is that the authors have been able to present complex information in a simple, clear and straightforward way. Thus, it helps us to develop our own frameworks and strategies.

I firmly believe that teaching social thinking and related skills to those who have weaknesses in the intuitive lifelong development of these skills is one of the most complex and challenging things to teach. Breaking down the skills and teaching them step by step as the authors of this book do is the key to success.

Michelle G. Winner, Speech Language Pathologist
Author of *Inside Out: What Makes a Person with Social Cognitive Deficits Tick?*
and *Thinking About You Thinking About Me*

introduction

The world around us is a complicated place filled with rules, guidelines, regulations, and policies. Although rules and mandates, in themselves, can be complex, most of us take comfort in them – often unconsciously – because they help us to know what to do in most everyday situations. Most of us like rules if they are consistent. It is when they are unclear, are used inconsistently or are unstated that we become upset, indignant or confused.

Brenda recently had an opportunity to make a presentation in a foreign country. She was the first presenter of the day and was to speak from the stage in a large auditorium. About 20 minutes prior to the presentation, she was on the stage doing last-minute preparations – making sure her computer worked, the projection system was aligned to the screen, the volume was working on the DVD player, and so on. Next to the computer where Brenda was to present stood a chair and a small table that held a pitcher of water and a glass. Having finished checking everything out, Brenda sat down in the chair to wait. Suddenly, an announcement came over the public address system, "Dr. Brenda Myles, please get off the stage." Confused, Brenda jumped up and quickly ran to sit in the audience. Apparently, she had violated an unwritten rule or protocol dictating that *all speakers are to be introduced from the audience and then move to the stage.*

We are surrounded on a daily basis by such unstated rules or customs that make the world a confusing place. This is known as the **hidden curriculum**.

The purpose of this book is to make readers aware of the hidden curriculum, its elusiveness, and its impact. Some of us require more instruction in the hidden curriculum than others. Some seem to learn the hidden curriculum or aspects of it almost automatically. Others learn the hidden curriculum only by direct instruction. And that is where this book comes in. After a general introduction to the nature of the hidden curriculum, a series of instructional strategies will be presented that can be used to teach the hidden curriculum. Finally, extensive, but not comprehensive, lists of hidden curriculum items or unstated guidelines are offered. Due to the elusive nature of the hidden curriculum, the lists – while broad – offer samples rather than a definite set of lessons to be learned. Parents, educators, and others are encouraged to consider the lists as springboards to making their own lists geared specifically toward the unique needs of the person with whom they are working or living and the given situational contexts.

What is the "Hidden Curriculum"?

The hidden curriculum refers to the set of rules or guidelines that are often not directly taught but are assumed to be known (Garnett, 1984; Hemmings, 2000; Jackson, 1968; Kanpol, 1989). The hidden curriculum contains items that impact social interactions, school performance, and sometimes safety. The hidden curriculum also includes idioms, metaphors, and slang – things most people "just pick up" or learn through observation or subtle cues, including body language. For example, to most a term such as "get off of my back" and accompanying body language (frowning, looking irritated, raising voice) communicates that the speaker wants to be left alone, but to somebody who has social-cognitive challenges and predominantly interprets language literally, the term will have a totally different meaning and be very confusing.

If the hidden curriculum is assumed knowledge, you may ask, how can we determine the items that comprise it? This question points to one of the greatest difficulties about the hidden rules – it is difficult to explain all the rules, but when they are broken, they become painfully clear. Therefore, one of the primary ways to recognize an example of the hidden curriculum is when a hidden curriculum error occurs. Certain phrases are indicative that a hidden curriculum item has been violated. For example, if you are ever tempted to say to a loved one, friend, or student any of the following, you are probably referring to a hidden curriculum item:

- *I shouldn't have to tell you, but …*
- *It should be obvious that …*
- *Everyone knows that …*
- *Common sense tells us …*
- *No one ever …*

Breaking a hidden curriculum rule can make a person a social outcast or certainly a social misfit. For example, there is a hidden curriculum for nose picking. It is not *"do not pick your nose."* Rather, it is *"pick your nose in the bathroom and use a tissue."* Failure to follow the hidden curriculum can cause a child to be shunned by peers, be viewed as gullible, or considered a troublemaker. Another example of a hidden curriculum item is: *"When someone asks, 'do you have the time?' the person does not want a yes or no response; he or she wants to know what time it is at that given moment."* The child who unknowingly replies "yes" to this question about time might be punished for purposefully being rude or disruptive. In many cases, the child is neither, but is simply interpreting the question literally.

The Elusiveness of the Hidden Curriculum

The hidden curriculum is complex and elusive. Although we have attempted in this book to provide extensive lists of hidden curriculum items, we recognize that it is impossible to identify all such items. What complicates matters further is that you cannot blindly accept all of the hidden curriculum items because many variables come into play in a given situation that influence whether the hidden curriculum item will work for you, a loved one, friend, or student.

For example, the phrase "shut up" can be interpreted in several different ways. When used between two teenage girls engaged in friendly conversation, "shut up" can mean "amazing" or "wow." But between two girls who are angry with each other, the term can mean that the speaker wants the other person to be quiet, to quit talking.

Reading the Hidden Curriculum of Body Language

Body language is about how we communicate or "speak" with our body. It includes gestures, facial expressions, body posture, and tone of voice. Understanding a person's body language is an important aspect of being able to develop relationships and communicate effectively. Sometimes body language seems different than a person's words, and for this reason, it is important to understand body language.

For example, a person who says that he likes you but frowns at the same time might in reality not really like you. A student can often tell if a teacher is angry by the tone of his voice and the way he crosses his arms rather than the words he uses. Sometimes body language is the best way to understand how someone feels. Table 1 gives some examples and interpretations of body language.

Table 1		
Examples of Body Language		
Body Part	**Action**	**Interpretation**
Head	Leaning to one side	Not understanding, listening, thinking
Face	Scowl (involves whole face: eyes are narrowed and squinted, nose is wrinkled, lips are pressed together, mouth is sometimes to one side)	Displeasure, intimidation, bullying, anger
Eyes	Wide open	Surprise, amazement
	Almost closed ("open just a slit")	Disbelief, doubt
	Looking straight at someone or something (for longer than a glance)	Staring (which is considered rude)
Eyebrows	Pulled close together (sometimes referred to as "knitted brows")	Thinking, confused
Mouth	Corners of the mouth lifted up (smile)	Greeting, happy
	Corners of the mouth turned down	Sad, unhappy, disappointed
	Opened wide	Surprise, shock
Chin	Lifted, pushed forward	Proud, tough, defiant
Body	Pointing a finger	Giving directions, threat, getting in trouble
	Hands on hips	Frustrated, bored, questioning/expecting an answer
	Shrugging shoulders	Questioning, don't know
	Arms folded across chest	Unapproachable, listening/taking in information

The Hidden Curriculum Differs Across Age

Another confounding factor about the hidden curriculum is that it changes depending the age of the persons involved. The hidden curriculum for a 9-year-old is different from that for a 16-year-old or a 25-year-old. Take, for example, the hidden curriculum item related to getting the attention of someone you like. If you are a 9-year-old boy, you can show that you like a girl by gently pushing her, following her around, pulling her ponytail, or making silly faces. What if you were a 16-year-old boy and engaged in those behaviors? In all likelihood, you would be instantly ostracized and called "a jerk." Worse yet, if you were 25 years old and did those things, you might be seen as a menace or as potentially dangerous. In fact, it is entirely possible that a 25-year-old in this instance might come to the attention of the police.

Similarly, many children like to play spy games. They eavesdrop on conversations by using mini-microphones and set up play alarms that go off when someone passes them. They also write notes to each other using secret code or invisible ink. This is appropriate at age 9 or 10. At age 18, it could be called stalking.

The Hidden Curriculum Differs Across Gender

Little girls routinely say to each other, "I like your shirt," "Your hair is pretty," or "Are you sure you are feeling okay?" What if a little boy were to make a similar statement to another boy? By the end of the lunch period, everyone at school would think that he was "weird."

While our society has moved toward gender equality and has attempted to do away with gender stereotypes, differences in manner and behavior still exist between males and females. Most of these are not directly taught, but if not understood, they can cause problems and misunderstandings.

The Hidden Curriculum Differs Depending on Who You Are With

If an adolescent is with an adult, his language is probably not "colorful" and may be somewhat grammatically correct. But if that same adolescent is with his peers (and no adults are in sight), a few curse words might "slip" into the conversation. Is cursing the right thing to do? Of course not, but it is typical of many adolescents, even "good kids."

Terry's mother, Mrs. Johnson, thought that her son, at age 13, should be taught the hidden curriculum for cursing. Terry had already learned many curse words incidentally and was getting in trouble for using them. His mother considered it natural for 13-year-old kids to curse on occasion and thought her son deserved this rite of passage.

She felt that she could not teach this hidden curriculum item because as a parent her job was to enforce the "no cursing" rule. So she talked with a friend in her neighborhood, Mrs. Smith, who also had a 13-year-old son and asked if her son, Rey, could teach Terry the hidden curriculum rules for cursing. Mrs. Smith agreed that this would be okay. The two mothers sat down with Rey and outlined the most "appropriate" curse words and gave him the hidden curriculum rule for cursing, "Look around first. If you see an adult, do not say any curse words. If you don't see an adult, it is probably okay to use the words in a sentence."

Does this mean that we should advocate teaching the hidden curriculum for cursing to every adolescent? No! What to teach is an individual decision. Mrs. Smith felt it was the right decision for her son. Other parents may differ, and that is their prerogative.

Cultures Each Have Their Own Hidden Curriculum

Understanding the hidden curriculum in cultures other than one's own can be difficult as illustrated in the *Introduction*. Many cultures have unstated rules involving eye contact, proximity, gestures, and ways of addressing people. Some cultures are high-context cultures, where nonverbal cues are more important than the words that are said. This is significantly different in low-context cultures where words, rather than nonverbal cues, express the real meaning of the conversation.

In some cultures belching loudly at the end of dinner expresses appreciation for a well-cooked meal. To most of us in the United States, such behavior is considered rude and embarrassing. Similarly, in Italy it is proper for a mother and her adult daughter to walk down the street holding hands. In the United States that behavior would be perceived as odd.

impact of the Hidden Curriculum

While some of the examples in this book may seem somewhat humorous, the impact of not knowing or following the hidden curriculum can be serious. A demonstration of not understanding the hidden curriculum can cause a child to be bullied, ignored, made fun of, or be misunderstood. Its impact can be felt in the school, community, home, on the job, or in the judicial system as described below.

School

Schools have their own multifaceted hidden curriculum – the unwritten culture of schools. How to dress, what type of backpack to carry, how to greet a fellow student, where to hang out between classes, what games are acceptable to play … the list goes on.

How do students know how to dress? They didn't attend a fashion class, they learned from observation. They observed the popular kids in school, their heroes in the movies, or studied the catalogues of favorite stores, and drew from these their personal style. Should everyone dress alike? No. Students should be able to express themselves in a manner that is comfortable to them (and within the bounds of school and parental acceptance or tolerance). However, students need to know the hidden curriculum in order to make an informed decision about their appearance.

Within the school, teachers also have their own hidden curriculum – often known as *teacher expectations*. While teachers develop and teach certain classroom rules, they do not teach the many expectations they have for their students. Almost universally, teachers say that they don't teach expectations because they are common sense, are obvious, or should have been taught years earlier. These expectations are the hidden curriculum and when unstated, they can make school a difficult place for some students.

Richard LaVoie (cited in Bieber, 1994) outlined hidden curriculum items that are not understood in the school setting or that teachers do not address in their classrooms. These include:

- What students should be doing when the bell rings

- Physical plan of the building. How to travel from class to class in the most direct way

- The administrative structure

- Which administrator is a "safe person" to talk with

- The daily schedule

- The intermural schedule

In brief, what most students "pick up" in the first couple of days is what should be taught to the students who do not understand the hidden curriculum, such as:

- Which teachers will tolerate lateness or tardiness?

- Which teachers give homework?

- Which teachers place value on final exams?

Home

The hidden curriculum at home often is related to the values and rules of the individual family.

Margaret has an 11-year-old son, Mark, who has Asperger Syndrome (AS). Although he loves his mother, Mark is not demonstrative – he does not hug her or tell her that he loves her on a regular basis. Because it was important to Margaret that she receive some positive attention from her son, she talked with Mark about the importance of telling parents that they are loved. Mark was flabbergasted that his mother would tell him this, exclaiming, "I told you that I loved you when was I four years old. Why should I repeat myself?" Margaret told Mark that mothers generally like to hear that they are loved frequently. When Mark asked for a schedule so that he could tell her on a regular basis, they decided that on every holiday he would say that he loved his mother.

Margaret hopes that Mark will become more spontaneous about expressing emotions, but until he does, he at least understands the hidden curriculum rule that parents like to hear that they are loved often.

At other times, the hidden curriculum is related to etiquette and tradition. Parents and caretakers often explicitly teach some hidden curriculum items as a typical part of parenting and at other times when they become aware that their children have deficits in these areas. However, these deficits sometimes only become apparent during times of stress and, as a result, children do not receive patient instruction, but instead are given a rule without explanation.

Karol is a 9-year-old girl with high-functioning autism who has a minor phobia about germs. One day her mother invited a new neighbor who had just moved to New Jersey from Japan to visit. When Sachi Hagiwara, the neighbor, arrived, she immediately took off her shoes. Aghast at this behavior because her family typically wore shoes in the house, Karol burst out, "Oh, great! We'll probably have to have the carpet cleaned before I can sit on it again." Karol's mother, who was embarrassed by her daughter's outburst, simply told Karol to be quiet.

Although her mother's response was typical of what most parents would do in similar circumstances, Karol required more support. She needed explicit instruction on why their visitor took off her shoes and the possible implications for transmitting germs.

Community

While home-related hidden curriculum items are often easily remedied by caretakers with little damage to self or others, errors made in the community may have more negative ramifications. Peter Gerhardt (personal communication, April 2004) talks about the hidden curriculum of urinals. For example, if there is only one man at a urinal, the hidden curriculum dictates that a newcomer not go to the urinal next to that person. Rather, he should go to a urinal that is at least two stalls away. Also, boys and young men should know that they are not to talk to someone while they are at the urinal and that they should never go to the bathroom in groups. Further, boys and young men should merely unzip to urinate rather than pulling down their pants at the urinal. Boys who pull down their pants could be open to victimization or be accused of exhibitionism.

On a totally different note, there is a hidden curriculum for going to the library with parents. This hidden curriculum dictates actions in the library as follows:

1. **Why are you at the library?** *To get a book.*

2. **How long are you there?** *Long enough to check out a book.*

3. **How loudly do you talk?** *Talk in a quiet voice or whisper.*

4. **Is it fun?** *It is tolerable, but not particularly fun.*

Parents generally teach this skill to children and youth with social-cognitive challenges, including those with autism spectrum disorders (ASD), who often have difficulties with the hidden curriculum, and provide careful guidance prior to going to the library and also while at the library. As these children get older, particularly in the middle school grades, they may be invited to the library by peers. The hidden curriculum is different for teens who go to the library, as illustrated below.

1. **Why are you at the library?** *Generally, the excuse is to check out a book or to study; however, it is actually a social activity, a time to hang out with friends, pretend to look at books, talk, laugh.*

2. **How long are you there?** *While parents may want to set a time limit, teens prefer to stay for several hours – until the library closes or they are kicked out.*

3. **How loudly do you talk?** *At the library, the teens talk as loudly as they can without being told to quiet down. It is also likely that loud giggling will occur.*

4. **Is it fun?** *Absolutely.*

Teens who do not know these hidden curriculum rules may be ostracized by peers in the library, as the teens with ASD follow the former routine: go to their favorite shelf of books, select reading material, announce that they are ready to leave, and prompt their peers to talk more softly.

Dating and other intimate relationships are also surrounded by a hidden curriculum that is very complex. Temple Grandin (1995), an internationally known animal scientist who is on the autism spectrum, has definite views about relationships, "Even today, personal relationships are something I don't really understand ... I make social contacts via my work. If a person develops her talents, she will have contacts with people who share her interests" (p. 139). In other words, Temple Grandin recognizes her challenges in this area and has made a deliberate choice to play it safe by staying within the comfort zone of her professional expertise and socializing with people who have similar talents and interests.

Many individuals who have difficulties with the hidden curriculum take a perspective other than Dr. Grandin's and venture beyond the safety of their special interests. If they do, they would do well to learn the specific aspects of the hidden curriculum that involve personal relationships. Some books that deal with how to develop personal relationships are listed under the heading "Other Materials That Can Be Used to Teach the Hidden Curriculum" in the chapter *Hidden Curriculum Items*. In addition, some basic guidelines are included on page 63 under Social Situations.

Workplace

Mastering the hidden curriculum in the workplace can present major obstacles. Many assumptions are made regarding understanding the hidden curriculum in a place of employment because adults are assumed to be knowledgeable about workplace mores and, if not immediately competent on these issues, to master them in a short period of time. In other words, there is even less tolerance, and therefore more serious conse-quences, for breaking curriculum rules in this context.

There are many hidden curriculum items to master in the workplace. For example, it is widely acknowledged in the business literature that two organizational charts exist in every company – one is written up in the company manual; the other, although not printed, is the chain of command that is actually followed. Individuals with social-cognitive challenges and related characteristics, who tend to be very rule-bound, might not discern this difference and be ostracized or targeted for not adhering to the accepted chain of command.

Other hidden curriculum issues in the workplace include:

- Can business email be used for personal correspondence?

- What does "casual business dress" mean?

- How do you know when it is timely to introduce a new idea?

- Is there someone at work who should be avoided?

- What is meant by "the customer is always right"?

- What do you do if you disagree with your boss?

- How do you ask for more responsibilities at work?

- How do you negotiate a raise?

- Do you go out to lunch or bring your lunch?

- What does "lunch hour" mean?

- Do you take a break at work? If yes, when, where, and for how long?

- How do you express anger toward a work colleague?

Legal System

The hidden curriculum surrounding law enforcement and the legal system is quite complex, and failure to understand or misunderstanding the rules can have severe ramifications.

Recently, an evening news show featured a young man who had been arrested. Obviously distressed, he was sitting in a room with three-way mirrors with a detective. The detective was questioning him – rapidly firing questions at him. At one point, the officer told the young man that if he would confess, he could go home. After only minor deliberation, the young man confessed to the crime, which he had not committed, so that he could go home as promised. Of course, that scenario did not occur; instead, the young man was incarcerated.

The hidden curriculum items that the young man did not know were many, including:

- Do not confess to a crime that you did not commit.

- Call a lawyer if you are being questioned by a law enforcement officer.

- Do not talk to the law enforcement professionals until the lawyer is present.

Dennis Debbaudt, in his book *Autism, Advocates, and Law Enforcement Professionals*, offers specific suggestions regarding the legal system for individuals with AS and other autism spectrum disorders based on his experiences as a police officer.

> *Independent persons [with a social-cognitive challenge] often ask about what they can do when approached by law enforcement professionals. Law enforcers have suggested proper identification, and a prepared handout that includes information that the person has [a social-cognitive challenge] and may not understand their legal rights, explains behaviors that may appear suspicious, and gives any critical medical information and phone numbers for an advocate or law enforcement contact person. Law enforcers also suggest keeping the following in mind:*
>
> - *Do not attempt to flee.*
>
> - *Do not make sudden movements.*
>
> - *Try to remain calm.*
>
> - *Verbally let the officer know you have [a social-cognitive challenge].*
>
> - *If unable to answer questions, consider the use of a generic or person-specific [a social-cognitive challenge] information card.*

- *Obtain permission or signal intentions before reaching into coat or pants pocket.*

- *Ask the officer to contact an advocate, if necessary.*

- *For the best protection of all involved, the person will either verbally or through an information card invoke the right to remain silent and ask to be represented by an attorney.*

- *If you are a victim or are reporting a crime, you do not need to have an attorney present to speak to the police, but you may want the police to contact a family member, advocate, or friend who can help you through the interview process. (pp. 101-102)*

It is essential that these hidden curriculum items be directly taught to individuals who do not innately understand this system. In addition, more basic information regarding law enforcement is needed. For example, it is essential to understand the cardinal rule of not arguing with a police officer even if she is wrong.

We know a young man who had an unfortunate run-in with a police officer that could have had a disastrous outcome. John, age 22, had never had contact with the police before. Typical of many young adults, John was exceeding the speed limit while driving to work one morning. As a result, he was pulled over by a police officer. The officer approached John, requested that he give him his driver's license, and told him to remain in the car. As the police officer walked back to his car to check John's record for prior violations, John drove off. He did not realize that he was supposed to wait for the officer – merely taking it literally that he was to remain in the car!

Teaching the Hidden Curriculum

nstruction is key to helping individuals with social-cognitive challenges understand the hidden curriculum as many do not learn these items incidentally. Because of the wide range of hidden curriculum items, it is essential that a variety of instructional strategies be available for educators, therapists, and parents to use. The techniques and strategies presented in the following pages provide a structure within which to teach or interpret the meaning of the hidden curriculum.

Safe Person

It is important for children as well as adults to feel comfortable asking for help in learning and understanding the hidden curriculum. They have to be taught the skills of knowing who is a safe person to ask and the types of questions to ask. A safe person can be a parent or sibling, an understanding teacher or counselor, a paraprofessional, a job coach, mentor, or a close trusted friend who would provide accurate, clear clarification to meanings of words, phrases, situations – anything to do with the hidden curriculum.

When deciding who would be a fitting safe person, the following characteristics should be taken into consideration:

1. Understands the individual's characteristics and perspective.

2. Respects the individual.

3. Able to listen without interrupting and judging.

4. Knows when to listen and when to offer advice.

5. Able to take the other person's perspective.

6. Able to problem solve without engaging in a power struggle.

7. Knows when to maintain a flat, matter-of-fact facial expression and when to be animated.

8. Understands the triggers and behaviors that may lead to a tantrum, rage, or meltdown.

9. Able to use problem-solving techniques, such as Situation-Options-Consequences-Choices-Strategies-Simulation or cartooning (see below and pages 28-29).

10. Able to set boundaries, when necessary.

To benefit from such a relationship, individuals seeking help must be taught to phrase questions in such a way that they gain the necessary information. Examples of ways to phrase questions are:

What does _____ mean?

Help me understand.

When (a person) says / does _____, what do (they) mean?

Show me a better way to . . .

In addition, the person seeking help must learn not to argue with the advice/clarification offered by the safe person (Meyer, 2004).

Situation-Options-Consequences-Choices-Strategies-Simulation

Jan Roosa (personal communication, 1995) developed the Situation-Options-Consequences-Choices-Strategies-Simulation (SOCCSS) strategy to help students with social disabilities understand social situations and develop problem-solving skills by putting social and behavioral issues into a sequential form. This teacher-directed strategy helps students understand cause and effect and realize that they can influence the outcome of many situations by the decisions they make.

SOCCSS is generally used following a social situation to help students understand or interpret what happened to them. Although designed as interpretive, the strategy can also be used to teach social skills. That is, teachers can identify problems students are likely to encounter and address them using SOCCSS so that students will have a plan before a situation occurs (Myles & Adreon, 2001; Myles & Southwick, 1999). The strategy can be used one-on-one with a student or be taught as a group activity, depending on the situation and students' needs. SOCCSS contains the following six steps.

SITUATION: After a social problem occurs, the teacher helps the student identify who, what, when, where, and why. Who was involved the situation? What actually happened? When did it happen? Where did the problem occur? Why did it happen? The goal is to encourage the student to relate these variables independently. However, at first the teacher assumes an active role in prompting and identifying, when necessary, the answers to the questions.

OPTIONS: At this stage, the teacher and student brainstorm several behavioral options the student could have chosen. Brainstorming means that the teacher accepts and records all student responses without evaluating them. Initially, the teacher usually has to encourage the student to identify more than one thing he could have done or said differently.

CONSEQUENCES: For each behavior option generated under OPTIONS, a consequence is now listed. The teacher asks the student, "So what would happen if you … *(name the option)*?" Some options may have more than one consequence. For example, if a student decides not to seek help from his teacher on an assignment, he could (a) earn a low or failing grade as well as (b) be punished by his parents for not completing an assignment. It is often difficult for students to generate consequences because of their difficulty determining cause-and-effect relationships. Role-play at this stage can serve as a prompt in identifying the consequence.

CHOICES: Options and consequences are prioritized using a numerical sequence or a yes/no response. Following prioritization, the student is prompted to select the option that she thinks (a) she will be able to do and (b) will most likely get her what she wants or needs.

STRATEGIES: This step involves developing a plan to carry out the OPTION identified earlier if the SITUATION occurs. Although the teacher and youth collaborate, the student should generate the plan. This is important because the student must feel that she has been the decision maker and is responsible for the plan.

Table 2

SOCCSS

Situation – Options – Consequences – Choices – Strategies – Simulation

Situation

Who: David and Tom.

When: At recess after lunch.

What: Tom pushed David when they were standing in line at the slide. Mrs. Smith saw them and had both of them sit out for the rest of recess.

Why: David started teasing Tom about the coat he was wearing.

Options	Consequences	Choice
Ignore David's comment.	David could continue to say mean things.	
	David might stop saying mean things.	
Avoid being around David at recess.	If David is playing on the slide, Tom would not be able to be there and he likes the slide.	
Tell David to stop, and if he doesn't, tell the teacher.	The teacher would tell David to stop.	✔ (Tom's choice)
	The teacher would tell Tom to ignore him.	
Say something mean back to David.	Tom would get in trouble by a teacher.	
	A teacher might not hear Tom.	

Strategy – Plan of Action

The next time that David says something mean to Tom, Tom will tell him to stop.

If David doesn't stop teasing Tom, Tom will tell the teacher.

SIMULATION: Practice is the last stage in SOCCSS. Roosa defined simulation in a variety of ways: (a) visually imagining carrying out the strategy, (b) talking with another person about the plan, (c) writing down the plan, or (d) role-playing. After the simulation, the student evaluates the simulation to determine whether he now has the skills and confidence to carry out the plan. If the answer is "no," additional simulation must take place.

Table 2 provides a copy of the SOCCSS worksheet that was used with Tom who had pushed another child, David, on the playground. This behavior occurred after David had teased Tom about the coat he was wearing.

The SOCCSS social decision-making strategy has broad applications for children and youth who have social-cognitive and related difficulties by helping them understand (a) cause and effect, (b) that choices exist for almost all social situations, and (c) that they can impact and predict the outcome of many situations themselves. In addition, its visual and static presentation allows the student adequate time to reflect on the problem-solving sequence and its solutions. SOCCSS can be used by parents, teachers, or therapists. Its versatility allows it to be used for many situations – at home, in the community, or at school. Finally, it is a low-tech intervention – all that is needed is a pencil and a piece of paper.

SOCCSS was the subject of two recent studies. Coupled with a conflict resolution curriculum, the strategy was used with two elementary-age boys with AS who experienced tantrums, rage, and meltdowns related to misunderstanding social situations. SOCCSS was modified in both studies by providing study participants with a list of options from which they could choose. Both students experienced success with SOCCSS although to varying degrees (Mehaffey, 2003; Trautman, 2003).

Seek-Observe-Listen-Vocalize-Educate

The Seek-Observe-Listen-Vocalize-Educate (SOLVE) strategy is an empowerment strategy for individuals with social-cognitive challenges. In fact, SOLVE can be viewed as more than a strategy – it is a way of viewing the world, or a special mindset. The great thing about SOLVE is that it can be used in almost all environments and situations (see Table 3).

SEEK: The hidden curriculum is multifaceted. We discover new hidden curriculum items every day so it is important to be on the lookout in every social situation for hidden curriculum items. That is, we must be active seekers and learners.

OBSERVE: Observation is one example of how we can learn about the hidden curriculum. Taking time to evaluate a social situation before interacting with others is often an easy way to identify the hidden curriculum. Watch how peo-

Table 3
SOLVE Strategy

S	**Seek**	Seek to understand all aspects of the hidden curriculum.
O	**Observe**	Observe what people are doing and NOT doing.
L	**Listen**	Listen to what people are saying and NOT saying.
V	**Vocalize**	Vocalize … ask questions, check for understanding.
E	**Educate**	Educate … teach and learn. Remember: knowledge is power.

ple act toward each other; watch their movements; watch to see whether they join in a group or if they stand alone. All of these observations can help understand the hidden curriculum better.

LISTEN: Pay attention to what people are talking about. Are they talking about work, a movie, mutual friends, music, books, a concert, or a television show? Attend to what people are saying so that you can join in the conversation in a way that will be enjoyable to everyone. In this context it is just as important to identify what people are not talking about. For example, at company parties, attendees do not usually talk about work. If you were in that situation, it would be important to be aware not to talk about your job the whole time.

VOCALIZE: If you are unsure what a slang term, idiom, or gesture means, ask someone quietly to explain it to you. Similarly, if you don't know what to wear to a specific social event – ask. A safe person – someone you respect and like – can provide assistance in such situations. If you don't ask, you may not understand the hidden curriculum and end up in an uncomfortable situation, being misunderstood, ostracized, or worse.

EDUCATION: By now you know a lot about the hidden curriculum. If you see someone who is struggling to understand the hidden curriculum, you may want to help by explaining a hidden curriculum rule. Remember, however, that it is sometimes hard for people to take advice from others. If you are a safe person for an individual, she will probably want your help. If you are not, look to see whether your advice is needed or wanted. This may be done by asking, "Can I help you?" or you could make a helpful statement such as, "The last time I went to this type of [*fill in the name of the event*], I didn't know that ... [*fill in the hidden curriculum item*].

Social Narratives

Social narratives provide support and instruction by describing social cues and appropriate responses to social behavior and teaching new social skills. Written by educators or parents at the child's or person's instructional level, and often using pictures or photographs to confirm the content, social narratives can promote self-awareness, self-calming, and self-management (Myles & Simpson, 2003). Few guidelines exist for creating social narratives other than to ensure that the content matches student needs and takes student perspective into account (see Table 4). Figure 1 is an example of a social narrative.

Table 4

Guidelines for Constructing Social Narratives

1. **Identify a social situation for intervention.**
   The author of the social narrative selects a social behavior for change, preferably one whose improvement can result in positive social interactions, a safer environment, additional social learning opportunities, or all three.

2. **Define the target behavior for data collection.**
   It is necessary to clearly define the behavior on which data will be collected. The behavior should be defined in such a way that the student and everyone who will be collecting data understand it.

3. **Collect baseline data on the target behavior.**
   Collecting data over an extended period of time allows for determining a trend. Baseline data collection can last from three to five days or longer.

4. **Write a social narrative using language at the child's level. Consider whether to use first-person ("I") or second-person ("you") language.**
   Social narratives should be written in accordance with the student's comprehension skills, with vocabulary and print size individualized for each student. The author must decide whether the social narrative would be more effective if it is written with "I" statements (e.g., I need to remember to ...) or "you" statements (e.g., You need to remember that ...). The narrative can be constructed using present or future tense (to describe a situation as it occurs or to anticipate an upcoming event, respectively).

5. **Choose the number of sentences per page according to the student's functioning level.**
   For some students, one to three sentences per page is adequate. Each sentence allows the student to focus on and process a specific concept. For others, more than one sentence per page may result in an overload of information such that the student does not comprehend the information.

6. **Use photographs, hand-drawn pictures, or pictorial icons.**
   Pictures, such as photographs, hand-drawn pictures, or computer-generated icons, may enhance understanding of appropriate behavior, especially with students who lack or who have emerging reading skills or are visual learners.

7. **Read the social narrative to the student and model the desired behavior.**
   Reading the social narrative and modeling related behaviors as needed should become a consistent part of the student's daily schedule. The student who is able to read independently may read the narrative to peers or adults so that all have a similar understanding of the targeted situation and appropriate behaviors.

8. **Collect intervention data.**
   The author should collect data using the procedures described for collecting and analyzing baseline data.

9. **Review the findings and related social story procedures.**
   If the student does not respond with the desired behavior approximately two weeks from the introduction of the social narrative, the author should review the narrative and its implementation procedures. If program alterations are made, it is recommended that only one variable be changed at a time (e.g., change only the content of the story rather than simultaneously changing the time the story is read *and* the person who reads it). By changing only one factor at a time, it is possible to determine the factor(s) that best facilitate(s) a student's learning.

10. **Program for maintenance and generalization.**
    After a behavior change has become consistent, it is recommended that the social narrative be faded. Fading may be accomplished by extending the time between readings or having students be responsible for reading the story themselves. In some cases, the social narrative is not faded. This decision should be made on a case-by-case basis.

Figure 3
Social Narrative

Helping Myself

Sometimes I like to have people (especially my mom) do things for me.

My mom is not a waitress OR a taxi driver OR a maid. I can NOT order her or anyone to do things for me. That is rude, and people will not like my behavior if I do that.

I must do things for myself. I am not helpless. I am smart and very capable. I will do things for myself first.

I will only ask someone to do something for me if I am not able to do it myself, not because it is easier to have them do it – like fixing me something to eat, turning on the TV or covering me up.

If I need help, I will ask in a polite tone using words that are kind and respectful. Sometimes people will say "yes" and help me. I will remember to say "thank you." But sometimes they will say "no," and that is okay too. I might feel frustrated or disappointed inside, but I will use polite words when I speak. I will NOT keep asking the same question over and over or ask "why." Instead, I will say "okay" or "yes, ma'am" or "yes, sir." Then I can choose to do it myself or not do it at all.

Social stories. The most frequently used social narrative is Social Stories™ (Gray, 1995, 1998; Gray & Gerand, 1993). A social story is an individualized text or story that describes a specific social situation from the student's perspective. The description may include where and why the situation occurs, how others feel or react, or what prompts their feelings and reactions (Gray, 1998; Gray & Garand, 1993). Within this framework, social stories are individualized to specific situations, and to individuals of varying abilities and lifestyles. Social stories may exclusively be written documents, or they may be paired with pictures, audiotapes, or videotapes (Swaggart et al., 1995). They may be created by educators, mental health professionals, and parents – often with student input.

Although social stories have gained widespread recognition and popularity (Myles & Simpson, 2001), only two studies have empirically measured the efficacy of using this strategy with individuals with social-cognitive difficulties but without cognitive disabilities (Bledsoe, Myles, & Simpson, 2003; Rogers & Myles, 2001). Both investigations resulted in positive behavior change.

Cartooning

Visual symbols such as those found in cartoons often enhance social understanding by turning abstract and elusive events into something tangible and static that a person can reflect upon (Dunn, Myles, & Orr, 2002; Hagiwara & Myles, 1999; Kuttler, Myles, & Carlson, 1998). Visual systems may enhance the ability of children and youth with social-cognitive challenges to understand their environment, including the hidden curriculum (Gray, 1995; Rogers & Myles, 2001).

One type of visual support is cartooning. This technique has been implemented by speech/language pathologists for many years to enhance their clients' understanding. Cartoon figures play an integral role in a number of other intervention techniques, including pragmaticism (Arwood & Brown, 1999), mind-reading (Howlin, Baron-Cohen, & Hadwin, 1999), and comic strip conversations (Gray, 1995). Each of these techniques promotes social understanding by using simple figures and other symbols, such as conversation and thought bubbles, in a comic strip-like format.

Comic strip conversation. Perhaps the most commonly used cartooning strategy is Gray's (1995) comic strip conversation. Gray (1994) provides a structure by which to create comic strip conversations.

ENGAGE IN SMALL TALK: Before discussing the problem situation, the adult and child should engage in small talk. Small-talk discussions, which include drawing figures, are typically not focused on the problem situation. Rather, the teacher uses this opportunity to strengthen rapport and build confidence between himself and the student. Small-talk topics could include the weather or weekend activities.

DRAW ABOUT A GIVEN SITUATION: Gray (1994) recommends that the student draw the comic strip conversations; others (Bledsoe et al., 2003; Rogers & Myles, 2001) report that the student is better able to relay information about the situation if the teacher draws as the child talks. Either way, artistic ability is not required; stick figures work just as well as more intricate drawings if they are labeled so everybody involved knows who the cartoon figures represent. An adult guides the student's drawings by asking a series of questions that provide detail for the student's cartoon such as, Where are you? Who else is there? What did you do? What did others do?

PRESENT PERSPECTIVE: The adult shares her personal insights during the cartooning process when a natural opportunity occurs. Gray (1994) stresses that students should have as much control as possible during the cartooning session and that the adults should strive "to achieve a balance between gathering insights into the student's perspective, while sharing accurate social information" (p. 9).

PROVIDE SEQUENCE OR STRUCTURE: Gray (1994) recommends providing comic strip boxes in which the students can draw figures, particularly if they have organizational problems. Comic strip boxes can be numbered and easily reordered if the events are drawn out of sequence.

SUMMARIZE THE CARTOON: This step allows participants to synthesize the comic strip conversation in chronological order. The student should verbalize independently or as much as possible, with the adult clarifying only as needed. Summarization ensures that both the child and the adult have the same understanding of a given situation.

IDENTIFY NEW SOLUTIONS: The adult and student work together, again with the student performing as independently as possible, to identify new outcomes of the pictured event. These solutions should be written to allow for student reflection. The adult and student jointly analyze each item, discussing the advantages and disadvantages of each. The student retains this list, which becomes her plan for future situations.

Cartooning has limited scientific verification. However, some evidence suggests that learners with AS, for example, may be good candidates for social learning based on using a comic strip format to dissect and interpret social situations and interactions (Howlin et al., 1999; Rogers & Myles, 2001). Figure 2 shows a cartoon used with a child with AS to teach non-literal language use.

Figure 2
"How's It Hanging Dog"

Developed by Elisa Gagnon. Used with permission.

Power Card Strategy

The Power Card is a visual aid that uses a child's special interest to help her understand social situations, routines, the meaning of language, and the hidden curriculum. The Power Card strategy consists of a script and a Power Card (Gagnon, 2001).

> **SCRIPT:** The script is a brief scenario written at the child's comprehension level that utilizes his or her hero or special interest in addressing the behavior or situation that presents challenges. Specifically, the script discusses the child's hero or model, who experiences a problem similar to the one experienced by the child. A statement that contains a rationale for why the positive behavior is needed for the hero or model is also included. A brief three- to five-step strategy is then presented in the script outlining the problem-solving method used by the hero or model, including a description of how the hero experiences success with this strategy. This solution is ultimately generalized back to the child, and a note encouraging the child to try the new behavior (i.e., the one used by the hero or model that resulted in a positive outcome) is written into the script. The script may include pictures or graphics of the special interest, such as magazine pictures, computer-generated photographs, teacher or student drawings, or icons.

> **POWER CARD:** The Power Card, the size of a business card or trading card, contains a picture of the special interest and a summary of the solution. Designed to be portable to promote use across multiple environments and eventual generalization, the Power Card can be carried or can be velcroed inside a book, notebook or locker. It may also be placed on the corner of a child's desk (Gagnon, 2001).

This strategy has been empirically investigated with two children. In one case, the Power Card strategy resulted in marked behavior change and generalization across settings (Keeling, Myles, Gagnon, & Simpson, 2003). In a second study the child experienced moderate success when the Power Card strategy was used (Myles, Keeling, & Van Horn, 2001). Figure 3 shows a Power Card script and a Power Card used to teach a 9-year-old how to handle frustration.

Social Autopsies

Lavoie (cited in Bieber, 1994) developed the concept of social autopsy to help students with social problems understand social mistakes. Similar in format to SOCCSS, social autopsies are designed to dissect a social error to understand its components. With the student as an active participant, this verbally based strategy typically begins with an adult asking, "What happened?" The adult proceeds to ask clarifying questions to ensure that she and the student share the same knowledge base. Once this information

Figure 3
POWER CARD Strategy

Geoffery is a 9-year-old boy with Asperger Syndrome. His special interest is French cooking. He wants to be a chef when he grows up. If he does not understand what he is expected to do, he becomes frustrated (quickly pacing around the room, becoming verbally aggressive and refusing to listen to what people are trying to explain).

Using a hero based on his special interest (a chef with the French name Jean-Paul), Geoffery's Power Card gives him four options, or appropriate choices, to help calm himself, bringing him back to a teachable level.

SCRIPT
Being a French chef is fun. It is exciting to cook new foods. Yet sometimes Chef Jean-Paul gets frustrated, especially when he does not understand the directions of a recipe or what his assistant is explaining to him. He used to get upset and yell at people or not listen to them when they tried to tell him things. But he realized this was not the best way to handle his frustrations.

Instead he has learned several ways to self-calm. He wants to share these ideas with you. If you start to get upset, just try one of the following. If you still are upset, try a different one.

1. Take 5 deep breaths, exhaling slowly after each breath.
2. Close your eyes and slowly count from 1 to 20.
3. Listen to your favorite CD with your headphones on.
4. Go to a quiet place and look at cooking magazines.

Corresponding POWER CARD

Chef Jean-Paul wants you to remember to choose one of the following ways to help calm yourself:

1. Take 5 deep breaths, exhaling slowly after each breath.
2. Close your eyes and slowly count from 1 to 20.
3. Listen to your favorite CD with your headphones on.
4. Go to a quiet place and look at cooking magazines.

is gathered, the student is prompted to (a) identify the error, (b) determine who was harmed by the error, (c) decide how to correct the error, and (d) develop a plan so that the error does not occur again.

A social skills autopsy is a constructive problem-solving strategy designed to decrease the likelihood that similar social misunderstandings will reoccur. One of the tenets of social autopsies is that they be conducted in a timely manner just following the event. Because a student may encounter social misunderstandings in a variety of environments, every adult with whom he or she has regular contact, such as parents, bus drivers, teachers, custodians, and cafeteria workers, should know how to do a social skills autopsy. Generally held in a one-on-one session, social autopsies provide an opportunity for a student to actively participate in analyzing his social interactions.

According to Lavoie (cited in Bieber, 1994), "The autopsy process is particularly effective in enabling the child to see the cause/effect relationship between his social behavior and the reactions of others in his environment" (p. 11). Lavoie further states that the success of the strategy lies in its structure of practice, immediate feedback, and positive reinforcement. The script of a social autopsy conducted by a teacher with a child appears in Figure 4.

Figure 4
Social Autopsy

Remember Karol, the 9-year-old girl who had a phobia about germs? When the neighbor (recently from Japan) took her shoes off in the house, Karol reacted by saying, "Oh, great! We'll probably have to have the carpet cleaned before I can sit on it." Karol's mother told her to "be quiet" when instead she should have said "excuse me" to the neighbor and explained to Karol (through a social autopsy) what happened and what she could have done instead.

Clarify through:	**Example:**
1. Asking, "what just happened?" Everyone needs to have the same knowledge base.	Mom asks Karol to explain the situation from her perspective to have a clear understanding. Then mom "walks" Karol through the social "mishap," explaining to Karol about Sachi Hagiwara's custom of removing her shoes.
2. Identifying the error.	Karol's comment about the germs and having to have the carpet cleaned.
3. Determining who was harmed by the error.	Sachi Hagiwara was embarrassed and possibly offended. Mother was also embarrassed.
4. Deciding how to correct the error.	Karol should apologize to Sachi Hagiwara for any embarrassment she might have caused by making the comment the way she did.
5. Developing a plan so that the error does not occur again.	Karol could do one of the following: • Think the comment inside her head but not say it out loud. • Tell the person in a polite voice that she can keep her shoes on. • Leave the room.

Direct Instruction

Direct instruction is a teacher-led model that includes frequent interactions between teacher and students. These interactions may be scripted with a text for teachers to follow and indicators suggesting when student responses should be solicited. In direct instruction, a brisk pace is maintained, with the teacher modeling correct behaviors while soliciting student responses to ensure understanding. Students respond frequently using a variety of verbal and physical response modes, including verbalizing an answer, writing down an answer, or role-playing. As for other strategies, immediate feedback is an important component of direct instruction. Following a verbal response or role-play, students receive specific feedback that reinforces accurate responses and provides additional practice for skills not mastered at a 90-95% accuracy rate. Curricula by Baker (2003) and Winner (2000) can be helpful in this regard.

An Item a Day

The hidden curriculum covers an infinite number of items, so teaching and mastering them can seem overwhelming to teachers and learners alike. By approaching the task based on the saying, "A journey of a 1,000 miles begins with a single step," it seem less daunting.

If a teacher begins each day of school by overviewing one hidden curriculum rule and calling it to the attention of students when she sees its occurrence, a child can learn 180 items each year. Likewise, if parents present one item each evening as the child is going to bed or during breakfast in the morning, the child can be introduced to 365 additional hidden curriculum examples. Thus, with little effort, children and youth can learn 548 pieces of information a year that will allow them to be more successful and happier in their social interactions.

Incredible 5-Point Scale

Buron and Curtis (2003) created the Incredible 5-Point Scale to help individuals with social-cognitive challenges learn to better understand their emotions and reactions to events in their lives and, eventually, independently modulate their responses. The scale is unique in that it can be used as an obsessional index, a stress scale, a meltdown monitor, and so on.

Using the scale, children and youth are taught to recognize the stages of their specific behavioral challenges and learn methods to self-calm at each level. Figures 5 and 6 provide illustrations of how the Incredible 5-Point Scale may be used.

The Incredible 5-Point Scale

Control This!

Colton is in the fourth grade. He has Asperger Syndrome and has had problems getting along in school since he was in kindergarten. He likes to be in control and gets upset if he perceives that something is "wrong." For example, if someone cuts in line he may feel compelled to punish that person by kicking or hitting him.

Curiously, Colton's ability to control his aggressive response to others' behavior seems to vary greatly from day to day. One day he may not be bothered by another student taking two milks at lunch. The next day the same offense may be too much for him to handle and he may end up kicking the offending child. Colton's mother does not work outside the home, so she is able to come to the school and pick him up when he becomes aggressive.

The team decided to help Colton by using a 1-5 point scale to teach him to recognize his own ability to "control" his reactions. Using the scale, he started to check in with the principal four times a day to rate his level of control. If he rated himself at a 4, he would have an alternative recess (like playing chess with the principal) and eat lunch in the classroom with a friend rather than in the less structured and noisy cafeteria. If he rated himself a 5, he would call his mother, who would come to pick him up before he lost control.

This program would not work if Colton did not like school, but he loved school, so he did not rate himself at a 5 very often. He was also very rigid and did not like to stay home because that meant a change in his day. He enjoyed recess and liked playing hockey, so he didn't rate himself a 4 unless he was very close to getting into trouble.

The program has not eliminated Colton's aggressive behavior, but it has helped him understand his lack of control. It has also helped the team realize that he needed more supervision and support in large social settings.

26

Control This!

Name: Colton			Control This!
		My Control	Scale
Rating	Looks like	Feels like	I can *try* to
5	Kicking or hitting	My head will probably explode	Call my mom go home
4	Screaming at people Almost hitting	Nervous	Go to see Mr. Peterson
3	Quiet sometimes rude talk	Bad mood grumpy	Stay away from kids (The ones I don't like!)
2	Regular kid - not weird!	Good	Enjoy it while it lasts
1	Playing hockey	A million bucks ¢	Stay that way!

29

Learning About Control

Control is a funny thing. It helps to learn more about it and about myself.

It's okay to want to be in control. Being in control can make you feel more relaxed about things.

Sometimes I have lots of control. I am relaxed and feeling good.

I call this being at a 1.

Sometimes I have some pretty good control. I can usually make a good choice when I have pretty good control.

I call this being at a 2.

Sometimes I don't feel great. I may not even want to be at school. Maybe I just don't feel like talking.

On these days I don't have really good control.

I call this being at a 3.

Sometimes I get up on the wrong side of the bed!

I am grumpy on those days and may not be able to make very good choices.

I wouldn't call this very good control – in fact, I almost don't have any control.

I call this being at a 4.

27

The Incredible 5-Point Scale

Then there are those really, really bad days.

They don't happen very often but when they do, look out!

Sometimes I just lose all control.

I can't make good choices and sometimes I am in danger of hurting someone else.

This is being at a 5.

It is good to learn about control so I can learn to be more independent, successful, and capable!

Figure 5
From: The Incredible 5-Point Scale (pp. 26-29) by K. D. Buron and M. Curtis, 2003. Shawnee Mission, KS: Autism Asperger Publishing Company. Used with permission.

I'm 6'2", Strong as an Ox – So Can You Tell Me Why I'm Trembling?

"I'm 6'2", Strong as an Ox – So Can You Tell Me Why I'm Trembling?"

David was referred to the self-contained high school program after being expelled from his home high school. He had broken several windows in the school cafeteria and the glass entrance/exit door nearest to the cafeteria. As a result, he had been to juvenile court and was placed on probation.

David identified his behavior as self-defense. "It was like my head was going to explode because of all the noise and confusion in the cafeteria. It's always confusing, and today there was a food fight. I had to do something to make it stop, I was afraid my head was going to explode."

The rating scale that follows does not rate David's level of anger, but his fear. David told us he feels afraid when he is "confused" so when developing this scale, we discussed things that we were afraid of, and David drew pictures to help him understand his own fear.

The Incredible 5-Point Scale

Understanding My Feelings by David

Scared/Afraid

My word for this is:
trembling

This is how I look:

This is how my body feels:

This is what I do:
Hide.

This is what I say:
"I've got to get out of here!"

Things that David says make him "tremble":
  "When I get confused."
  "When it is loud and crowded."
  "Catastrophes like tornadoes and earthquakes and war."

42

I'm 6'2", Strong as an Ox – So Can You Tell Me Why I'm Trembling?

Name: **David**   My Scared/Afraid/Trembling   Scale

Rating	Looks/Sounds like	Feels like	Safe people can *help*/ I can try to
5	Wide-eyed, maybe screaming, and running, hitting.	I am going to explode if I don't do something.	I will need an adult to help me leave. Help!
4	Threaten others or bump them.	People are talking about me. I feel irritated, mad.	Close my mouth and hum. Squeeze my hands. Leave the room for a walk.
3	You can't tell I'm scared. Jaw clenched.	I shiver inside.	Write or draw about it. Close my eyes.
2	I still look normal.	My stomach gets a little queasy.	slow my breathing. Tell somebody safe how I feel.
1	Normal – you can't tell by looking at me.	I don't know, really.	Enjoy it!

43

Figure 6
From: The Incredible 5-Point Scale *(pp. 41-43) by K. D. Buron and M. Curtis, 2003.*
Shawnee Mission, KS: Autism Asperger Publishing Company. Used with permission.

Video Modeling

In video modeling children and youth learn a hidden curriculum item or other skills sets by observing a videotape of themselves or others engaging in a task or completing an activity.

Video self-modeling. Video self-modeling (VSM) involves a child watching himself perform a task on video. For example, when learning the hidden curriculum item regarding greeting different types of people (i.e., teachers, students, community officials), the student might be videotaped while role-playing various greeting scenarios with a peer or adult. The student would then view the videotape and see himself engaging in the appropriate activities (Bellini, 2003). There are two types of VSM: positive self-review and video feed-forward (Dowrick, 1999).

Positive self-review (PSR) is used with children or youth whose behavioral repertoire once included a specific skill, but who do not perform the behavior any more. The child would be videotaped performing the behavior with assistance (i.e., cueing or prompting) from an adult or peer. The assistance would then be edited out of the videotaped scenario so the child could view herself engaging in the skill independently. In this manner, PSR serves as a refresher for the student (Dowrick, 1999).

Video feed-forward (VFF), on the other hand, serves as an instructional tool for the student who knows the component parts of a skill, but cannot put the behaviors together into a cohesive whole.

> *Manuel has learned the steps to introduce himself to a peer. He is to (a) approach a student, (b) look at the student, (c) say "hello," (d) check to be sure the other person is attending to him, (e) say, "My name is Manuel," and (f) then make a comment related to something he has in common with his peer ("I heard you like Matchbox 20" or "Did you see Spy Kids 3-D?"). Manuel can do these skills in isolation and in role-play, but has difficulty completing the sequence on the playground at school or in the community. VFF, for Manuel, would involve taping him engaging in each of the six behaviors in isolation. Then the tape would be spliced to show the sequence occurring in an orderly manner.*

Video instruction. Another type of video modeling, video instruction (VI), involves providing children and youth support by viewing others engaging in a specific behavior or performing a certain task. VI may be used to show a child a series of skills in isolation and then combined in the way they would be used in "real life." In addition, VI may be used to review a previously acquired skill that is not used consistently, similar to positive self-review.

> *Keisha and her family were getting ready to go to their annual family reunion. To ensure that Keisha has a successful experience, her Aunt Martha videotaped the inside and outside of the house where the family reunion is to be held. On the videotape Aunt*

Martha told Keisha what activities will be available at the family reunion and what kind of food will be served. In addition, she showed pictures of family members who were going to be at the reunion. Keisha and her family watched the videotape four times, so that she would be comfortable at the family reunion.

Teaching someone to read a person's body language has to be done in social contexts. Watching videos is a great way to teach someone how to interpret body language. You can stop the video, critique the movement or gesture, rewind, show it again, and so on. Observing conversations, watching facial expressions, hand gestures and body posture as well as role-playing what a person is saying or not saying is also a way to teach the hidden curriculum of body language.

According to Bellini (2003), there are several advantages to using VSM or VI:

- It supports learning using the child's visual learning style.

- It is motivating.

- Video modeling is proactive; it allows a child to examine a social situation before a problem occurs.

Video modeling has been used successfully with children with a variety of needs, including those with attention deficit hyperactivity disorder, selective mutism, social anxiety, and ASD (Charlop-Christy & Daneshvar, 2003; Charlop-Christy, Le, & Freeman, 2000; Charlop & Milstein, 1989; Harvey, Clark, Ehlers, & Rapee, 2000).

Summary

Each of the strategies reviewed here can be effective in teaching the hidden curriculum. Regardless of the technique used, it is important to understand that these essential rules, mores, and manners must be taught and become a part of the repertoire of the individual with social-cognitive challenges.

Hidden Curriculum items

While we recognize that it is impossible to identify all of the hidden curriculum items that lead to life success, on pages 43-71 we have compiled lists that will be useful as you plan formal instruction. We hope that reading these items will help you to identify others that may be essential to children and youth who don't innately understand the hidden curriculum.

Readers need to keep in mind that the hidden curriculum items presented here are general guidelines of what to do or what not to do. As discussed earlier, they may differ based on who you are with, where you are, the interpretation or perspective of those involved, and so on. It is always a good idea for those learning the hidden curriculum to discuss these items with adults they trust. The hidden curriculum items are organized around the following major topics:

- Airplane Trips
- Bathroom Rules
- Birthday Parties
- Clothing
- Eating
- Friendship

- Life Skills
- School
- Social Situations
- At the Swimming Pool
- Figurative Speech and Idioms
- Slang Terms

Other Materials That Can Be Used to Teach the Hidden Curriculum

The ideas presented in this book can be supplemented with other materials that address issues surrounding the hidden curriculum. The following is a brief list of books that may be used to teach children and adolescents unwritten rules. Parents and teachers may want to preview the books before using them to ensure they teach the hidden curriculum items you want your children and students to know.

Practical Solutions to Everyday Challenges for Children with Asperger Syndrome (Myles, 2002). Written specifically for children with Asperger Syndrome ages 5-11 by a nine-year-old, this practical book covers many of the innumerable everyday occurrences that can complicate the lives of children with autism spectrum disorders. The following sections are particularly relevant: school-related, getting along, emotions and concerns, and miscellaneous.

How Rude! The Teenager's Guide to Good Manners, Proper Behavior, and Not Grossing People Out (Packer, 1997). This book covers everything from getting along with peers to using "netiquette" (online etiquette). The book is fast-paced, entertaining, and written in teenager-friendly language.

Bringing up Parents: The Teenager's Handbook (Packer, 1992). On the surface, this book appears to teach adolescents how to manipulate their parents to get what they want. In reality, Packer provides instruction on communicating clearly, being an active listener, taking responsibility for one's actions, negotiating, and comprising. Topics include solving family problems, communicating effectively with parents, and coping with sibling issues.

As a Gentleman Would Say: Responses to Life's Important and Sometimes Awkward Situations (Bridges & Curtis, 2001). Although this book is directed toward men (and male adolescents), it applies equally well to women (and female adolescents). The book begins with 53 Things Every Well-Spoken Gentleman Knows, including how to listen, how to ask for favors, and understanding the meaning of "no." It also covers a diverse range of items related to lending and borrowing, dining out, meeting new people, and funeral behavior protocol.

A Little Book of Manners for Boys (Barnes & Barnes, 2000). In this book Coach Bob talks to boys about being a good sport, taking care of things, eating, and other important issues. The book is written for boys between the ages of 6 to 12. Parents can read one item per day to a child and discuss it at the dinner table or at bedtime.

A Little Book of Manners: Courtesy and Kindness for Young Ladies (Barnes, 1998). This colorful book features Aunt Evelyn and Emilie, who discuss telephone, mealtime, part, playtime, and visiting manners, among other topics. The book is structured as a series of short vignettes that can be read by or to a child.

How to Behave: A Guide to Modern Manners for the Socially Challenged (Tiger, 2003). Designed for older adolescents and adults, this book covers travel by planes, trains, and automobiles; big-city living; leisure time; dating and love; and out on the town. It covers real issues that we often encounter, but for which many of us are not prepared. For example, lane blocking, tailgating, cutting others off, blocking, and merging when driving are clearly discussed.

The American Girl series by Pleasant Company. This series of books are invaluable to girls of all ages. The books feature lifelike, attractive illustrations and use language that is informal, but informative. Books in the series include *The Care and Keeping of You: The Body Book for Girls* (Schaefer, 1998), *I Can Do Anything: Smart Cards for Strong Girls* (Kauchak, 2002), *Writing Smarts: A Girl's Guide to Writing Great Poetry, Stories, School Reports, and More!* (Madden, 2002), *The Feelings Book: The Care and Keeping of Your Emotions* (Madison, 2002), and *Staying Home Alone: A Girl's Guide to Feeling Safe and Having Fun* (Raymer, 2002).

Life Lists for Teens (Espeland, 2003). This book is a great resource for teens of all ages. It covers an extensive array of topics about life experiences, how to get along, learn and have fun.

Summary

How-to books and other informational material can be valuable aids in teaching individuals the hidden curriculum. Books such as those listed above as well as the *Idiot's Guides* and the *Dummies'* guide books, despite their unfortunate titles, can be excellent and fun-to-use resources.

Lists of Curriculum items

Airplane Trips

- When riding on an airplane, use only one armrest. If you are sitting in an aisle seat, it is usually best to use the armrest on the aisle side.

- Avoid placing any part of your body over the armrest and into another's seating area.

- Soft drinks and snacks are usually free on airplanes.

- Do quiet and sedentary activities during the flight (reading, computer, writing, etc.).

- If you are playing a video game or walkman/MP3 player/iPod, turn the audio volume off or wear headphones. Make sure that your MP3 player, iPod, etc., is powered up before the flight.

- The temperature on an airplane may not be comfortable for you. Think about wearing or bringing a light-weight shirt and jacket/sweatshirt.

- When listening to music, sing quietly to yourself, not out loud.

- Unless you are in the aisle seat, try to limit the number of times you leave your seat.

- Airlines usually do not provide a variety of food during a flight. It is best to bring a small snack if you think you will get hungry and have specific tastes.

- No one is allowed to smoke on an airplane.

- Do not tell the person sitting next to you that he is too fat for the seat.

- When sitting in your seat, do not push, pull, or kick the seat in front of you.

- Sit in your seat facing forward, not backward, regardless of who is sitting behind you.

- Remember to keep your feet on the floor and not on the back of the seat in front of you.

- Never joke about hijacking the airplane or harming someone on the airplane.

- Never joke about carrying guns, knives or bombs when at the airport or on the plane.

- Sometimes airplanes are not on schedule. The only thing that you can do is to calmly accept the change.

- If the airplane you are on has to stay temporarily parked on the runway, do a quiet activity to help pass the time.

Bathroom Rules

- Always wash your hands after you use the restroom.

- Make sure that you flush the toilet after you use it.

- Always close the door when using the restroom.

- When using the toilet, go in the toilet, not on the toilet. If you go on the toilet by mistake, wipe the toilet seat with unused toilet paper.

- Pull up your pants before coming out of the stall.

- Do not talk about what you did in the bathroom.

- For girls: Learn which toilets you can sit on and which toilets are better to squat over, or use a paper seat cover. It is generally a good idea to squat over or place a paper seat cover on toilets in public places or those that don't appear clean.

- For boys: Don't talk to others around you when using the bathroom.

- For boys: When using the urinal, instead of pulling your pants down, just unzip them, pull out your penis, urinate and put your penis back in your pants and zip them up.

- For girls: Do not talk to the person in the next stall, unless she is a friend of yours.

- When entering the bathroom, do not look through the separations between the stall doors to see if a stall is empty. Look under the stall door, towards the bottom of the toilet. If you see someone's feet, use a different stall.

- Do not write on the bathroom walls (even if others do).

- Avoid complaining to the person who just came out of the bathroom that she made it stink.

Birthday Parties

Before the Party

- Do not ask to be invited to someone's party.

- The birthday party may not be celebrated on the actual day of the birthday.

- If you are around people who are not invited to a party, do not discuss plans for the party around them.

- Buy a present for the person that he would like – not something that you would like.

At the Party

- The host/birthday girl or boy is the "boss."

- If you are a teenager and the party is an all-girl party, the topic of conversation may be about boys.

- You may not like the theme of the birthday party – people have different interests and tastes. If you do not like the theme, do not tell the host.

- While you are at a birthday party, avoid talking about your last birthday party and how much better it was.

The Birthday Cake

- Only the birthday person can blow out her candles, unless she invites somebody to help out.

- You may not like the design on the cake, but don't say that the cake is ugly.

- If you do not like the flavor of the cake, you may simply say, "No thanks" or "I don't care for any right now" when offered a piece.

- Wait until the birthday person blows out the candles and the cake is cut before you eat a piece of cake.

- If the birthday person is older, there will be many candles on the cake. Refrain from saying things like "The cake is as bright as the sun" or "I need my sunglasses."

- Sometimes you may not like all of the food that is offered at the party. Do not tell the host that the food is bad. In declining, just say, "Maybe I'll eat something later," "Not right now, thank you," or "I am not hungry right now."

Presents

- The person whose birthday it is gets to unwrap the presents by himself.

- Do not announce how much the present costs.

- Only the person who receives the present can play with the present, unless she gives you permission.

- Don't make rude comments about the gifts others gave the birthday person.

- When you give a gift that you had previously owned to someone, do not tell her that you did not want it any more.

- Refrain from telling someone you do not like his gifts.

- If you get a present that you already have, don't say, "Oh, I've already got five of these. Where can I take it back?" Instead, you can say something like, "This is a great gift – it is so good that I already have one." You can exchange it later.

- If you know what a person is getting for his birthday, do not tell him. Just say that you cannot share that information because it is a secret. It is not a lie to keep this kind of information secret.

Clothing

- Pajamas should not be worn outdoors.

- When you are out in public, a proper place to fix undergarments is in the bathroom stall. Do not pull on your underwear to "fix" them unless you are in the bathroom or another private place. Also, do not adjust your private parts in public.

- Untie your shoes before you try to put them on.

- It is inappropriate to take your clothes off in public even if you are hot.

- Wear clothes that are appropriate for the weather conditions.

- It is inappropriate to take your jeans off at school even if you are really hot or the jeans are uncomfortable.

- It is not cool for boys to wear pink underwear.

- Do not wear clothes so tight that people can see the line of your underwear through your clothes.

Eating

Basic Rules

- Wash your hands before eating meals and snacks.

- Always chew your food with your mouth closed.

- Put your napkin on your lap, not under your chin.

- Do not eat someone's food without asking.

- Use your own utensils to eat with – do not grab utensils from another person's plate.

- Use a tissue, not your napkin, to blow your nose.

- Do not blow your nose at the table. Excuse yourself and go to the bathroom to blow your nose.

- If you have to cough or sneeze, cover your mouth and move your head a little bit away from the table. When finished, wrap the tissue and put it in your pocket, then say "excuse me."

- After eating, refrain from leaning back in your chair and rubbing your stomach.

- Do not put ketchup or other condiments on everything you eat. This may gross out other people, and they may not want to sit by you next time.

- Do not brush your hair at the dining table.

- Keep food in your mouth at all times. Avoid taking a bite of food and spitting it back onto the plate, even if you do not like it.

- Burping out loud is not appropriate when eating.

- Use your own cup when you want a drink – do not drink out of a cup that is not yours.

- "Zapping" or "nuking" something means to heat it up in the microwave, not blowing something up with an atomic bomb.

Eating at a Friend's House

- When eating at a friend's home, wait until the head of the house says the food is ready. Do not go to the kitchen to see what is for dinner and ask when the food is going to be ready.

- Eat what you are served if there are no choices. If you do not like what is being served, say, "Just a little bit, please; I'm not very hungry" instead of "I don't want anything – I don't like it."

- If the host offers more and you are full or don't like the food, say, "No thank you, I'm fine," instead of "It was disgusting."

- When asked, "How is your meal?" be polite even if you did not like the food. It is kind to say, "Thank you for cooking such a nice meal" or "Thanks for inviting me to dinner."

- Know what the rule is for leaving the table. In some homes, a child may not leave the table until the head of the family is finished eating and leaves the table. In other families, a child may ask to be excused when he is finished eating. It is okay to ask the adults what the rule is.

Eating at a Restaurant

- When eating out, excuse yourself politely to go to the bathroom. You may have to ask the waitress where the bathrooms are.

- Learn about the dress code before going to a fancy restaurant. Don't wear jeans to a fancy restaurant.

- Refrain from talking about other people sitting next to you – do not comment on what they are eating or drinking, or what they look like.

- Use a quiet voice in the restaurant. You do not have to whisper – just talk in a low-volume voice.

- Do not talk with food in your mouth.

- Do not start eating until everyone has been served. When everybody else at your table starts eating, you may start.

- If finished eating, wait patiently for the others at your table to finish.

- Take small bites and eat slowly.

- When you are in a nice restaurant, conversation should not include stories that contain the word "blood" or stories that might be considered to be gross or gory.

- Do not ask anyone preparing the food in a public place when the food inspector is coming to check the kitchen.

- Do not tell the waitress that her hair is messed up.

- When eating out, place your napkin on your lap or keep it on the table.

- Appetizers are a part of the meal that people typically share. Do not eat all of the food on the appetizer plate. Make sure everyone who wants some gets some.

- When leaving the restaurant, never pick up money left on the table.

Buffet Lines

- Get a clean plate for each trip you make to the buffet.

- Never touch food on the buffet with your hands.

- If you drop something at the buffet table, leave it there.

- Wait until you sit down at your table before you start eating your food.

- Remember to use your fork and spoon, and possibly knife.

- Always use a napkin to wipe your face and hands, especially before you make a second trip through the buffet line and before you leave the restaurant.

Fast-Food Restaurants

- Don't wait to be seated at a fast-food restaurant.

- Wait in line to place your order.

- Learn how to order something in a fast-food restaurant.

- People have to clean their own tables and throw away their own trash at fast-food restaurants.

- When you get carryout food, do not turn the container of food on its side or upside down as the food may spell out.

Miscellaneous Rules

- When eating in a group, but not at a restaurant, it is polite to offer someone else some of your food or drink if you have enough.

- At the grocery store, it is okay to eat food when someone offers you something to try as part of a sample or taste test. If it is a sample or taste test, just try one piece. You cannot just try anything that you want without paying for it.

- Only take small helpings of food when eating "family style." Allow everyone to eat at least one serving before you help yourself to all of one item.

- If you are making a shake with a blender, make sure that there are no objects in the blender (like a spoon). Also, make sure the lid is on tight.

Friendship

Making Friends

- Friendship takes a lot of time to develop. Just because someone in your class was nice to you one time, it does not mean that he or she is your best friend.

- You should not have to pay somebody to be your friend.

- If someone never asks you to play, it is probably not a good idea to ask him to play every day.

- When you want to play with someone, do not pressure or nag at her if she tells you she cannot play.

- Do not play in other people's backyards unless you are invited.

- Just because a person is very popular, it does not mean that he is nice or a good person to have as a friend.

- When you are getting to know someone and want to invite the person to your house, consider doing a structured activity first, such as going to a movie or playing mini-golf. With these types of activities, there is a definite starting and ending time and you don't have a lot of time to talk.

- When you invite someone over to your house, you can alternate what you both want to do. For example, you can both do something that your guest wants to do first, then you can both do what you want to do.

Building a Friendship

- Friends tell each other secrets and their likes and dislikes. Friendship is different from just meeting someone on the street and talking to them.

- Friends say nice things to each other, not nasty comments like "You are fat."

- It is okay to be mad at your friend sometimes. Tell you friend politely that what he did made you mad and try to work out your differences. Sometimes it is okay "to agree to disagree."

- Friends forgive each other for mistakes they accidentally make.

- When you meet your friend's parents for the first time, do not tell them about problems you are having or secret things you did with your friend.

- When you go to someone's house, don't kick off your shoes, lie on the couch, and help yourself to food from the refrigerator unless you have been told by the people there that you may.

- Try not to ask your parents if a friend can stay for supper in front of your friend. It is embarrassing to the friend and your parents if they say no.

- If and when you sleep over at a friend's house, you may not always be on a bed and you may not be sleeping in an area by yourself.

- When you spend the night with someone, you should follow her routine, not your normal home routine. It is okay to ask her questions if you are not sure of what to do.

Life Skills

In the Community

- It is important to learn how to calculate and receive correct change from a clerk in a store.

- If you are short-changed in a restaurant or store, calmly tell the waiter or clerk that you did not receive the correct change before putting the money away or leaving. Tell them what type of money you gave them (e.g., two dimes and one nickel, two ones) and how much change you were expecting. In most cases, the short-changing is an accident.

- When you get on an elevator, always stand facing the doors; do not face the back or sides of the elevator, or stare at others.

- Whisper when inside a movie theatre.

- When other seats are available in the theatre, leave a space between yourself and a stranger.

- Do not say "fire" in a movie theatre.

- Clap after a play, not a movie.

- Although Ferris Bueller in the movie climbed on top of the railing at the Sears Tower skydeck, you should not do this! It could get you kicked out or badly hurt.

- It is a good general rule not to do in real life what people do on television or in the movies.

- When out in the community, hold doors open for someone older than you or when someone is close behind you.

- If someone gets hurt at a ballgame, it is a sign of support when people clap – not applause.

- At sporting events, it is normal to stand and cheer throughout the game. Do not stand the entire time unless everyone else does.

- When you see a sign that states "Garage Sale" or "Yard Sale" with an address, it does not mean that the people are selling their garage or yard. They are selling items that they do not want or need any more.

- In a department store, it is okay to cut in line to ask one question when other people are making purchases. Wait to the side by the cashier and ask your question when the cashier is ringing up the customer or waiting for the customer to pay. Do not interrupt a conversation.

- When trying on shoes in a store, wear socks or borrow some from the store employees.

- When someone standing in the street asks you for money, you do not have to give him money. You do not have to tell him how much money you have. The person may look like she needs money; you still do not have to give any. If you want to give money, do not give away all of your money. You could say, "I don't have any to give" or "This is all I can give you." (This does not apply to muggings. In a mugging, a criminal wants your money or possessions. It is best to give all of your money to a mugger to avoid getting hurt.)

- Do not tell the man at the grocery store that he is big and fat even if you think he is.

- While in the doctor's waiting room, do not ask people why they are waiting to see the doctor or tell them in detail why you are there.

- At a piano concert, school play, or similar event, try not to say "Is this ever going to end?" or "She doesn't play very well!" or anything else that the performer may find offensive.

- When at a small formal ceremony where someone is being recognized, do not hoot and holler unless everyone else does. Look to see what the audience does and follow along – like looking towards the person, listening quietly.

- When you lose something in a store and cannot find it, ask for the lost and found department, which is usually in the customer service area of the store.

- Be on your best behavior when in public.

Religious Worship, Including Funerals

- Whisper or use a low-volume voice in worship services or at funerals.

- Do not shout hello to your friend two pews ahead of you during religious services.

- During a funeral service, do not laugh out loud or make jokes about the person who died or anything else.

- Wear conservative clothing when going to a house of worship.

Car Care and Driving

- The Do Not Drive on the Shoulder sign means that you cannot use the shoulder (side) for a road, but if you need to pull over or your car breaks down, you can drive on the shoulder to slow down or stop your car.

- When buying a car, most of the time the price that is listed on the sticker is not what you pay for the car. Try to talk the dealer into a lower price than what is on the sticker.

- Even though it is true that hot water can melt ice, never pour hot water on your windshield when there is ice on it. This could crack or even shatter the windshield.

- Do not crawl over the seat in a car to get to the other side.

- Never argue with a police officer if you are pulled over. Do not argue, even if you think you are right.

- If someone pulls out in front of you when driving, try not to get angry. Honking the horn lightly may be okay.

- Learn the rules about the colors of the lines and dotted/solid lines down the middle of the road.

- If you are in the wrong lane and have to turn, go around the block instead of trying to get into the correct lane if there is traffic.

- When you get in or out of a car, keep your feet off the seat.

- Try not to block an entrance or exit to a business when you are stopped on the road. If a person is waiting to get onto the road you are traveling on, it is courteous to let that person out.

- If another driver is driving below the speed limit, do not honk your horn or make obscene gestures.

Talking on the Telephone

- Do not walk up and start talking to someone who is talking on the telephone.

- When taking a phone message, especially from a business, it is important to write down the name, number, time of call, and what the person wants. It is okay to ask the caller to repeat what he or she said or to talk a little slower.

- When you answer the phone, say "hello" and before you hang up say "goodbye."

- Do not call people on the phone early in the morning or late at night.

- It is not okay to make prank phone calls.

Pranks

- If you think you may want to tee-pee someone's house, find out the consequences. In some places, you can get a fine or be taken to jail.

- It is not a prank, if someone gets hurt. If you hurt someone, it is meanness.

Personal Issues

- Do not talk about how mucus looks or feels in the throat or looks in your tissue.

- Blow your nose discreetly rather than standing in the middle of a room and making a scene.

- Don't sneeze in your hand and then shake hands. Wash your hands first.

- Attend to your personal appearance (runny nose, wet clothes, etc.).

Visiting Friends

- When you walk up to or past someone's house, don't look in through the windows or doors.

- If you are knocking on the door or ringing the doorbell and nobody answers the door, leave and come back later. Do not let yourself in even if the door is open or unlocked.

Walking in Public

- When walking with someone, walk alongside the person. Don't leave him or her by walking ahead.

- Walk with your hands down to your side.

- Sometimes we have to walk quickly, but sometimes it is okay to go slow.

- If you have to get past someone, say, "Excuse me." Do not push people out of the way.

School

Bathroom Issues

- Ask permission or get a pass before leaving the classroom to use the bathroom.

- Quietly tell the teacher or an adult you need to use the restroom instead of announcing it to the whole class.

- Do not announce or discuss bathroom issues upon returning to class.

- Avoid yelling to another student that he forgot to zip his zipper. Tell the person quietly.

- If you need special bathroom supplies, you can usually get them from the school nurse.

Locker Room Rules

- It is appropriate to fix your hair and look at yourself in the mirror before and after P.E.

- If there are people taking showers or changing their clothes, do not stare at them or make comments about their bodies.

- Change into your P.E. clothes in the locker room, not the hallway.

- It is not appropriate to use other people's locker items without asking and receiving permission first, even if they are you friend.

- When you are taking a shower in a group setting, it is not appropriate to sustain eye contact or watch others take showers.

- It is not appropriate to touch others in the restroom or shower.

- Follow what the crowd does to know when it is appropriate to shower.

- Learn where to change clothes and if total nudity is appropriate.

Recess and P.E.

- Learn the rules of the games played at recess or P.E. If necessary, ask the recess teacher or P.E. teacher to explain.

- If you are throwing a ball to someone in the gym or at recess, say her name out loud and wait until she looks and has her hands out before throwing it.

- When playing tag, touch the other person softly as if you were petting a dog.

- If you lose a game at recess, it is okay. Usually the reason you play the game is to learn new skills or enjoy time with other people, not to win all the time.

- On the playground, students must share the equipment.

- When playing a game with teams, realize that everyone likes to have a turn. Encourage your teammates by saying positive, polite words, giving "high fives," and staying on the same team.

- During hide-and-seek, count to 10 while your eyes are closed before starting to look.

- When the whistle blows, it is usually time to line up from recess.

- It is okay to be loud on the playground. When it is time to go back inside, it is time to be quiet.

Lockers and the Hallway

- You may get bumped in a crowded hallway. It is usually an accident.

- When walking up and down stairs, stay on the right side and try not to crowd the person in front of you.

- If you have older or younger siblings at school, do not yell and be angry at them when they are with their friends. It will embarrass them.

- Do not let people (friends, strangers or adults) store backpacks or other bags in your locker without seeing what is inside. Ask permission before looking in their backpacks or bags.

- Sometimes boys and girls will be standing by a locker, hugging and/or kissing. It is best to ignore them instead of making a comment or staring.

Lunchroom

- In the lunchroom, begin eating right away so you do not waste time.

- Talk in a low-volume voice in the lunchroom.

- Do not yell across the lunchroom to your friends.

- Avoid bringing tuna fish to school in your lunch. It smells, and kids sometimes won't want to sit by you.

- Never throw food in the lunchroom, even if other students do.

Fire Drills

- During a fire drill, go with your class to the nearest exit and get outside. This is not the time to go to the bathroom or even ask to go to the bathroom.

- Remember to be quiet. This is not the time to talk or ask questions.

- It is okay to cover your ears to drown out the sound of the alarm when you are exiting the building.

School Dances

- Ask, do not grab, a person if you want to dance with him. If he says "no," say "ok" and walk away.

Assignments and Homework

- If you are unable to complete your work at school, take it home to finish it.

- When the teacher says, "do your best," that means you should try your hardest. It does not mean that you will automatically get 100% on the assignment.

- Even though your assignment is complete, you will probably get more points for making your work as neat as possible.

- During class, learn when the teacher will allow you to work on your assignments. You can find this out by asking the teacher.

- During group assignments in class, everybody in the group is responsible for doing the work.

- If you think that the teacher made a mistake in grading your paper, politely ask if you can talk with him about it.

- If you finish an assignment before other students in the class, work quietly at your desk until the teacher says to stop.

- It is inappropriate to comment on other students' work quality, unless the entire class is discussing how they can improve their work.

- Find out the teacher's rules if you perform poorly on a test or project. Do not have a tantrum or meltdown. Doing poorly on a test usually means that you have to learn to study in a different way. Talk with your parents and teachers so they can help you.

- If I do not want to do an assignment, you can think that quietly inside your head. You still have to do it. If you say something out loud, you may get in trouble.

- If you have a book report to do and reading the entire book feels overwhelming, one option is to go to a bookstore and buy a condensed or abbreviated version to read. Then read the whole book. The reading will go much faster because you will know the plot.

- If you are not sure where to turn in your assignments, watch what other kids do or ask the teacher.

Library

- Use a whisper or low-volume voice in the library.

- Check out the books that you are interested in before taking them out of the library.

- If the book you want to check out is not in, see the librarian about placing it on reserve for you.

- Try not to stand over someone's shoulder when they are checking email.

Rules When Talking to the Teacher

- If you disagree with what a teacher is saying, politely say what you think and wait for an answer. If you still disagree, let it go.

- Use a pleasant voice when talking to teachers. They will respond to you in a more positive way.

- Talk to your teacher in a different way than you talk to your friends. Always use a polite voice when speaking to your teacher.

- Refrain from saying rude comments to teachers like "You are old" or "You look really tired today."

- Teachers do not know all of the answers. It is okay if they have to look something up or ask someone else.

- Teachers use nonverbal communication to send messages to students. Sometimes teachers look at students, stand close to them, or raise or lower their voice to get their message across. If you do not know what the teacher is trying to communicate, ask politely.

- After a teacher returns from maternity leave, tell her congratulations. Do not tell her that she is still fat even if she may look that way.

- If you talk to the principal, avoid telling her that if she listened better, more kids would like her.

- Never call your teacher a bad name to her face or when other adults are around.

Classroom Rules

- Place the cap back on any pen or marker that you have been using.

- Use your own supplies. If you have to borrow something, remember to ask. Never grab or take something without asking first.

- Adjust your voice level to an inside voice in the classroom.

- Raise your hand to get the teacher's attention.

- Raise your hand when the teacher pauses, instead of when he is in the middle of explaining something.

- It's okay to make a mistake – white-out or an eraser can be used.

- If someone is doing something in class that is bothering you or making you uncomfortable, ask them to please stop and explain why it bothers you. If they continue, tell an adult.

- Always keep your hands and feet to yourself.

- Be willing to try new activities and skills.

- When saying the Pledge of Allegiance or singing the Star Spangled Banner, refrain from talking or laughing. To help keep your attention on the flag, choose a star on the flag and stare at it while you are saying the pledge or singing.

- Walk inside the classroom; run outside on the playground if you feel like it.

- While working, look at your own paper or book.

- During silent reading, read in your mind, not out loud.

- Be on time to class.

- Make eye contact with the teacher to let him know you are listening. If you can't look him in the eye, look towards his face.

- During the school day you are only allowed to be in certain places of the school. Know which areas are accessible to students.

- Limit yourself to approximately five questions during a class period in one school day. If you continue to ask questions, it may bother the other students and the teacher.

- When you are assigned to a group, stay with that group until the teacher changes the arrangement.

- Do not draw violent scenes when drawing or coloring in school.

- Do not talk about guns or knives at school.

- In middle and high school, teachers often have different rules. It is important to know the rules for each teacher. If you don't agree with the rules, it will do you no good to say that they are not fair.

- When the teacher is giving a lesson, it is time to listen. You can talk about topics that you are interested in at a later time.

- If you have guest speakers in class, do not interrupt their speech by talking or asking questions. Ask questions at the end of the speech.

- Most teachers do not allow students to chew gum in school. Chew gum after school.

- Teachers give students transition statements – learn what your teacher uses so you can be ready to go to the next subject or activity. For example, teachers may tell you that you will be leaving in 5 minutes. That may mean 2 minutes or 10 minutes. You will not know the exact time, but at least you will know that you are leaving soon.

- If you pass notes in class to a friend, do it discreetly so the teacher does not catch you. Passing notes can get you in trouble. If you don't want to get in trouble, don't pass notes.

- You will probably be teased if someone sees you tasting glue at school.

- Keep personal information about your family to yourself during school.

- Even if other students write in their textbooks or on their desks, use a piece of paper instead so you won't get in trouble.

- When it is time to clean up, it does not have to be perfect. The janitor will come in after school to vacuum and do the final clean-up.

- When standing in line, make sure there is enough space for one or two people between you and the person in front of you.

Behavior

- If a teacher tells another student to stop talking, it is a good idea for you to also stop talking since the teacher has already expressed disapproval of talking.

- If you get in trouble once, it does not mean that your entire day is ruined.

- When someone else is getting in trouble, it is not the time to ask questions or show the teacher something.

- If the teacher crosses her arm and clears her throat, it means that she either wants the class to be quiet or to look up and get ready to listen to a direction.

- If your teacher gives you a warning about your behavior and you continue the behavior, you will probably get in trouble. If you stop the behavior immediately after the warning, you will probably not get into trouble.

Bullying/Tattling

- Learn when it is okay to tattle.

- If other students are teasing you, do not get mad and hit them. Tell an adult who can help you.

- If other students are fighting or bullying others, tell the teacher. If they are goofing around in a friendly manner or having pretend fights, do not tell the teacher.

- Do not tattle on what every student is doing wrong. It is up to the teacher to catch the students and reprimand them.

- If one of your classmates tells you to do something you think might get you in trouble, stop and think before acting. Friends do not ask other friends to do things that will get them in trouble.

- Do not pick on other students.

- If someone picks on you, tell the teacher.

Social Situations

What Not to Say or Do

- Do not tell others that they have bad breath even if they do.

- Do not make negative comments about anyone's outfit or hairdo.

- Do not yell out, "Someone farted and it stinks!"

- Do not pick your teeth or other body parts (ears, nose) in class or public areas.

- Do not pick your bottom in class even if it itches or your underwear rides up. Do this in the bathroom.

- Do not pick at scabs or play with them during class.

- When you are with people whom you do not know well, do not pass gas, pick your nose, or scratch a private body part.

- Do not explain to a person with a new puppy that the breed she bought has a terribly aggressive disposition.

- Do not tell a neighbor that her house is much dirtier than it should be.

- Do not cut in line when buying tickets for a movie or a concert.

Making Conversation

- Face the speaker and position yourself in his or her direction.

- Maintain eye contact while talking with people.

- Say the other person's name to get her attention before starting to speak.

- Discuss other topics besides only those that you are interested in.

- Take turns in conversation.

- Who you are with determines what you should talk about. For example, you can talk about a new CD with a friend. You probably would not do this with an adult.

- Others may not always agree with you or you may not agree with others when talking. That is okay.

- If you are not interested in what others are talking about, try to disguise your disinterest by smiling, nodding, and asking a question about the topic.

- When making conversation, avoid constantly telling others how good you are at something. This usually makes other kids avoid being around you.

- Even if you are really good at something, do not brag about it. If other people are talking about what they are good at, then you can share your talent.

- Wanting to know the answer to a specific question should not be more important than the feelings of the people around you who might be embarrassed by your question.

- Think about the words you are saying. Are they kind, nice or necessary?

- It is not polite to interrupt others while they are talking.

- You do not have to make a comment about yourself every time someone tells you a story about himself. If you do that, most people see you as a "know it all" and eventually stop telling you stories.

- Keep approximately an arm's distance away from the person you are talking with.

- If someone asks you a personal question, it is okay to say that you are uncomfortable answering.

- People usually pause to take a breath once in a while when talking. They may even wait a little bit before talking again. Sometimes, people take a little time to formulate a thought or study your reaction to what they're saying. This pause does not mean that they are done talking. Wait at least 5-10 seconds before talking if you are not sure they are done.

Relationships

- When you kiss someone, do not have gum in your mouth.

- When two people are standing close and speaking very softly, they are having a private conversation. Generally, do not join the conversation without asking first. If the people are two of your really good friends, you can probably join the conversation. If you are unsure what to do, it is best to ask.

- If a classmate of the opposite sex is nice to you, this does not mean that he/she is your boyfriend/girlfriend. Going around and telling your classmates and friends will make it very difficult to have relationships in the future.

- When you see someone in the hall at school or out in the community that you are attracted to, find a way to let the person know without going directly up and saying loudly, "You're cute!" This is embarrassing to the recipient of the comment.

Social Rules

- Always be on time.

- Knock before entering a room, except when entering your classroom or a room in your house (except the bathroom).

- Although it is OK to say "hi" to everyone you walk by in a small town, this could get you in trouble in large cities.

- People act differently in different situations. Sometimes people treat you differently when they are around certain people.

- Refrain from making negative comments; try to be as polite as possible.

- When people are crying or are angry, do not laugh as it will make them feel worse.

- When someone asks "How do you like my new _____," they usually really want you to tell them you like it. Even if you don't like it, try to find something positive to say.

- When you leave a situation or place, always say goodbye.

- It is appropriate to shake hands with a stranger; hugging is okay if the person is a friend.

- Do not hit other people.

- If someone intrudes into your space, ask him politely to move over without touching him.

- While it might be okay to cuss in private, it is not appropriate to do so in public, especially when adults are near.

- If you respond with no enthusiasm to someone who is talking with great enthusiasm, she will probably stop talking with you.

- When hearing someone speak using incorrect grammar, do not correct him every time.

- There are certain questions that you do not ask others (weight, age, income, religion) if you have just met them.

- When out in public, do not go up to a complete stranger and ask for a piece of gum even if you see that they have some.

- Many words have double meanings, like the word "key," for example. Sometimes "key" means a metal object; at other times it means a plastic credit card like a pass. When someone says to use a key in a hotel room or other place, keep this in mind.

- If you forget the name of someone you just met, say politely, "I'm sorry, I forgot your name." The person will usually respond back with his or her name.

- Sometimes people bend the truth a little if it means sparing someone's feelings. For example, if someone asks you if you like their shirt and you do not, it is probably best to say something like, "That shirt is great." Or "I really like the colors in your shirt."

- When you try to find a seat to sit in, make sure that someone else is not planning to sit there. One way to find out is to see if they left something on or near the chair to save the seat for when they return.

Social Rules for Teens

- If you are a boy, even though a particular girl band or a girl singer is cool, others will think it is strange if you try to imitate them.

- At school, most students wear different outfits every day.

- When walking in the hallway, singing a song aloud is inappropriate.

- Find out what music is cool. Opera or classical music is usually not cool when you are a teenager. Some kids do like opera or classical music, but they don't talk about it.

- If you like a boy or a girl, you often pretend that you do not like them at all.

- Once you are in middle school, it is not cool to hug and kiss your parents around friends. You can hug them when it is just your family at home or if you are leaving for a trip.

- Sometimes arguing with your parents even if you know you are in the right gets you into more trouble than if you said nothing.

- Do not point out "funny bumps" on people's faces or ask them if they have pimples or zits.

- Two people can have the same thing (CD, shirt, pants, etc.).

- Even if you think someone's hair is pretty, try not to touch it.

Telling Jokes

- Repeating the very same joke after someone else has said it to the class will make others laugh at you, not the joke.

- Jokes that you tell friends are usually different from the jokes that you tell adults.

- Do not tell inappropriate jokes to a group of girls if you are a boy, such as jokes about private parts, etc.

- If you do something funny, it is usually only funny once. If you do it repeatedly, it makes you look silly and goofy.

- You may hear and enjoy "dirty jokes." Dirty jokes are usually about sex. It is best to keep these jokes to yourself. Especially do not tell dirty jokes to the opposite sex. Also, jokes or arguments about religion and politics should be avoided.

- Some people laugh when they are making fun of someone. They are not laughing because they think that person is funny. Do not do this because it is hurtful to the person who is being made fun of.

At the Swimming Pool

Buying a Swimsuit

- Always wear underwear when you try on a bathing suit at the store before buying it.

- Never buy a white bathing suit because your skin will show through when the suit gets wet.

- Make sure the suit you wear is a suitable style for your body shape and size. Ask others if you are not sure.

At the Swimming Pool

- Change into your swimming suit at home or in the bathroom at the pool.

- Always wear sunscreen if you are in the sun. Everyone at the pool may not like using sunscreen – do not force others to wear it.

- Once you are on the deck at the pool, refrain from making loud comments about other people's bodies or bathing suits.

- Not everyone at the pool will be swimming. Some people like to lie out in the sun and tan.

- If someone accidentally splashes water on you, it is okay. If you do not like to be splashed, move away from the water or the person splashing.

- If you have to go to the bathroom while you are in the pool, get out of the pool and use the bathroom, not the outside shower or the pool.

- For females, if you are in the middle of your menstrual cycle, do not go into the pool unless you are wearing a tampon. If people ask why you are not swimming, tell them you do not feel like swimming.

- If you are thirsty from swimming, do not drink the pool water. Go to the water fountain or drink from the sink in the dressing room (unless there is a sign saying that the water is not for drinking), or buy some pop or water from the concession stand.

Rules to Live By

- Treat others with respect.

- Take responsibility for your actions.

- Wait, wait, wait.

- Breaking the law is never a good idea, no matter what your reason is.

- Seek out an adult if you are hurt or cannot handle a certain situation.

- Take care of other people's property as well as you take care of your own.

- Control your anger.

- Remove cords from electrical sockets by holding the plug and pulling gently.

Figurative Speech and Idioms

The following is a small, random sampling of the kinds of idioms and figurative language that cause difficulty for individuals with social-cognitive challenges, who tend to interpret language literally. For additional examples, please go to: http://www.freesearch.co.uk/dictionary.

Term	*Meaning*
Bite my head off	to speak to someone in a quick, angry way – usually for no good reason
Bite the bullet	to force yourself to do something unpleasant or difficult, or to be brave in a difficult situation
Buckle down and get busy	start working hard
Bull in a china closet	very careless in the way that they move or behave
Can't make a silk purse out of sow's ear	you can't make something good out of something that is naturally bad
Curiosity killed the cat	said to warn someone not to ask too many questions about something
Don't be smart	when you speak to other people in a way that shows a lack of respect
Down in the dumps	unhappy
Driving me crazy	making someone annoyed or angry
Eagle eye	somebody who sees very well and notices things
Feeling blue	sad
Fit to be tied	extremely frustrated/angry
Get it off of your chest	to tell someone about something that has been worrying you or making you feel guilty for a long time

Term	Meaning
Term	*Meaning*
Get out of my face	a rude way of telling someone that he or she is annoying you and should stop
Go fly a kite	used to tell someone who is annoying to go away
Have eyes in the back of your head	to know everything that is happening around you
Heart of gold	to be very kind and generous
How the cookie crumbles	said when something slightly unlucky has happened but it could not have been prevented and so must be accepted
I'm so mad I could split nails	very angry
In a pig's eye	something that is highly unlikely
In hot water	to be in or get into a difficult situation in which you are in danger of being criticized or punished
Knock it off	used to tell someone to stop doing something that annoys you
Mad as a hornet	very angry
Mad as a wet hen	very angry
Make a mountain out of a molehill	to make a slight difficulty seem like a serious problem
Monkey see, monkey do	to copy or imitate someone
Open mouth, insert foot	to say something by accident that embarrasses or upsets someone, including yourself
Out in left field	no clue/strange
Over the hill	to be too old, especially to do a particular job

Term	*Meaning*
Pulling my leg	to try to persuade someone to believe something that is not true as a joke
Pulling the wool over my eyes	to deceive someone in order to prevent them from discovering something
Put a lid on it!	be quiet
Put on your thinking cap	to think seriously about something
Quiet as a mouse	to be very quiet
Quit horsing around	stop behaving in a silly and noisy way
Roll with the punches	to be able to deal with a series of difficult situations
Running off at the mouth	to talk too much in a loud and uncontrolled way
See red	to become very angry
So hungry I could eat a horse	you are extremely hungry
Start the ball rolling	to do something that starts an activity, or to start doing something as a way to encourage others to do the same
Straighten up	to behave well after behaving badly
That cracks me up	to suddenly make someone laugh a lot
Tied up in knots because	your stomach is tight and uncomfortable because you are nervous or excited
Top dog	a person who has achieved a position of authority
Uptight	worried or nervous and unable to relax
Watch your p's and q's	to be very careful about how you behave
When donkeys fly	you mean that it will never happen

Term	**Meaning**
When it rains, it pours	said when one bad thing happens, followed by a lot of other bad things, which make a bad situation worse
Winding down	to gradually relax after doing something that has made you tired or worried
You crack me up	to suddenly laugh a lot, or to make someone else suddenly laugh a lot
You kill me	to amuse someone very much

Slang Terms

Term(s)	**Context/Definition**
Just chill!	Calm down, relax.
Phat, snap!	Cool.
Shut up!, Get out!, Go on!, No way! Get out of here!	You're kidding!, Really? I can't believe it. (Never said to adults.)
Talk to the hand 'cause the face ain't listening!	I do not want to listen to what you are saying.
Way!	Yes.

References

Arwood, E. L., & Brown, M. M. (1999). *A guide to cartooning and flowcharting: See the ideas.* Portland, OR: Apricot.

Baker, J. E. (2003). *Social skills training for children and adolescents with Asperger Syndrome and social-communication problems.* Shawnee Mission, KS: Autism Asperger Publishing Company.

Barnes, E. (1998). *A little book of manners: Courtesy & kindness for young ladies.* Eugene, OR: Harvest House Publishers.

Barnes, B., & Barnes, E. (2000). *A little book of manners for boys.* Eugene, OR: Harvest House Publishers.

Bellini, S. (2003). Making and keeping friends: A model for social skills instruction. *Indiana Resource Center for Autism Reporter, 8*(3), 1-11.

Bieber J. (1994). *Learning disabilities and social skills with Richard LaVoie: Last one picked ... first one picked on.* Washington, DC: Public Broadcasting Service.

Bledsoe, R., Myles, B. S., & Simpson, R. L. (2003). Use of a social story intervention to improve mealtime skills of an adolescent with Asperger Syndrome. *Autism, 7,* 289-295.

Bridges, J., & Curtis, B. (2001). *As a gentleman would say.* Nashville, TN: Rutledge Hill Press.

Buron, K. D., & Curtis, M. (2004). *The incredible 5-point scale: Assisting students with autism spectrum disorders in understanding social interactions and controlling their emotions.* Shawnee Mission, KS: Autism Asperger Publishing Company.

Charlop-Christy, M. H., & Daneshvar, S. (2003). Using video modeling to teach perspective taking to children with autism. *Journal of Positive Behavior Interventions, 5,* 12-21.

Charlop-Christy, M. H., Le, L., & Freeman, K. A. (2000). A comparison of video modeling with in-vivo modeling for teaching children with autism. *Journal of Autism and Developmental Disorders, 30,* 537-552.

Charlop, M. H., & Milstein, J. P. (1989). Teaching autistic children conversational speech using video modeling. *Journal of Applied Behavior Analysis, 22,* 275-285.

Debbaudt, D. (2002). *Autism, advocates, and law enforcement professionals: Recognizing and reducing risk situations for people with autism spectrum disorders.* London: Jessica Kingsley.

Dowrick, P. W. (1999). A review of self-modeling and related interventions. *Applied and Preventive Psychology, 8,* 23-39.

Dunn, W., Myles, B. S., & Orr, S. (2002). Sensory processing issues associated with Asperger Syndrome: A preliminary investigation. *The American Journal of Occupational Therapy, 56*(1), 97-102.

Espeland, P. (2003). *Life lists for teens.* Minneapolis, MN: Free Spirit Publishing, Inc.

Gagnon, E. (2001). *The Power Card strategy: Using special interests to motivate children and youth with Asperger Syndrome.* Shawnee Mission, KS: Autism Asperger Publishing Company.

Garnett, K. (1984). Some of the problems children encounter in learning a school's hidden curriculum. *Journal of Reading, Writing and Learning Disabilities International, 1*(1), 5-10.

Grandin, T. (1995). *Thinking in pictures and other reports from my life with autism.* New York: Vintage Books.

Gray, C. (1994). *Comic strip conversations: Colorful, illustrated interactions with students with autism and related disorders.* Jenison, MI: Jenison Public Schools.

Gray, C. (1995). *Social stories unlimited: Teaching social skills with social stories and comic strip conversations.* Jenison, MI: Jenison Public Schools.

Gray, C. (1998). *The advanced social story workbook.* Jenison, MI: Jenison Public Schools.

Gray, C., & Gerand, J. D. (1993). Social stories: Improving responses of students with autism with accurate social information. *Focus on Autistic Behavior, 8,* 1-10.

Hagiwara, T., & Myles, B. S. (1999). A multimedia social story intervention: Teaching skills to children with autism. *Focus on Autism and Other Developmental Disabilities, 14*(2), 82-95.

Harvey, A. G., Clark, D. M., Ehlers, A., & Rapee, R. M. (2000). Social anxiety and self-impression: Cognitive preparation enhances the beneficial effects of video feedback following a stressful social task. *Behavior Research and Therapy, 28,* 1183-1192.

Hemmings, A. (2000). The hidden curriculum corridor. *High School Journal, 83*(2), 1-10.

Howlin, P., Baron-Cohen S., & Hadwin, J. (1999). *Teaching children with autism to mind-read: A practical guide.* London: Wiley.

Jackson, P. (1968). *Life in classrooms.* New York: Holt, Rinehart, & Winston.

Kanpol, B. (1989). Do we dare teach some truths? An argument for teaching more 'hidden curriculum'. *College Student Journal, 23,* 214-217.

Kauchak, T. (2002). *I can do anything!: Smart cards for strong girls.* Middleton, WI: Pleasant Company Publications.

Keeling, K., Myles, B. S., Gagnon, E., & Simpson, R. L. (2003). Using the Power Card Strategy to teach sportsmanship skills to a child with autism. *Focus on Autism and Other Developmental Disabilities, 18*(2), 105-111.

Kuttler, S., Myles, B. S., & Carlson, J. K. (1998). The use of social stories to reduce precursors of tantrum behavior in a student with autism. *Focus on Autism and Other Developmental Disabilities, 13*(3), 176-182.

Madden, K. (2002). *Writing smarts: A girl's guide to writing great poetry, stories, school reports, and more!* Middleton, WI: Pleasant Company Publications.

Madison, L. (2002). *The feelings book: The care & keeping of your emotions.* Middleton, WI: Pleasant Company Publications.

Mehaffey, K. (2003). *The use of a conflict resolution curriculum in reducing rumbling and rage behavior in a student with asperger syndrome.* Master's thesis, University of Kansas.

Meyer, R. (2004). Being your own case manager. In S. Shore (Ed.), *Ask and tell: Disclosure for people on the autism spectrum* (pp. 107-142). Shawnee Mission, KS: Autism Asperger Publishing Company.

Myles, B. S., & Adreon, D. (2001). *Asperger Syndrome and adolescence: Practical solutions for school success.* Shawnee Mission, KS: Autism Asperger Publishing Company.

Myles, B. S., Keeling, K., & Van Horn, C. (2001). Studies using the Power Card strategy. In E. Gagnon, *The Power Card strategy: Using special interests to motivate children and youth with Asperger Syndrome and autism* (pp. 51-57). Shawnee Mission, KS: Autism Asperger Publishing Company.

Myles, B. S., & Simpson, R. L. (2001). Effective practices for students with Asperger Syndrome. *Focus on Exceptional Children, 34*(3), 1-14.

Myles, B. S., & Simpson, R. L. (2003). *Asperger Syndrome: A guide for educators and parents* (2nd ed.). Austin, TX: Pro-Ed.

Myles, B. S., & Southwick, J. (1999). *Asperger Syndrome and difficult moments: Practical solutions for tantrums, rage, and meltdowns.* Shawnee Mission, KS: Autism Asperger Publishing Company.

Myles, H. M. (2002). *Practical solutions to everyday challenges for children with Asperger Syndrome.* Shawnee Mission, KS: Autism Asperger Publishing Company.

Packer, A. J. (1992). *Bringing up parents: The teenager's handbook.* Minneapolis, MN: Free Spirit Publishing Inc.

Packer, A. J. (1997). *How rude! The teenager's guide to good manners, proper behavior, and not grossing people out.* Minneapolis, MN: Free Spirit Publishing Inc.

Raymer, D. (2002). *Staying home alone: A girl's guide to feeling safe and having fun.* Middleton, WI: Pleasant Company Publications.

Rogers, M. F., & Myles, B. S. (2001). Using social stories and comic strip conversations to interpret social situations for an adolescent with Asperger Syndrome. *Intervention in School and Clinic, 36*(5), 310-313.

Schaefer, V. L. (1998). *The care & keeping of you: The body book for girls.* Middleton, WI: Pleasant Company Publications.

Swaggart, B. L., Gagnon, E., Bock, S. J., Quinn, C., Myles, B. S., & Simpson, R. L. (1995). Using social stories to teach social and behavioral skills to children with autism. *Focus on Autistic Behavior, 10*, 1-16.

Tiger, C. (2003). *How to behave: A guide to modern manners for the socially challenged.* Philadelphia, PA: Quirk Books.

Trautman, M. (2003). *A conflict resolution curriculum with a student with Asperger Syndrome.* Master's thesis, University of Kansas.

Winner, M. G. (2000). *Inside out: What makes a person with social cognitive deficits tick?* San Jose, CA: Author.